Personal, Social and Emotional Development

Sara Stocks

Contents

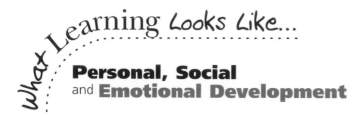

About this book

This book takes a close look at the area of learning which is concerned with children's personal, social and emotional development. In England and Northern Ireland, this is called Personal, Social and Emotional Development; in Scotland, Emotional, Personal and Social Development; and in Wales, Personal and Social Development. The author has taken, as a starting point, the goals or targets set down by the various curriculum bodies: the QCA (Qualifications and Curriculum Authority) in England; the Curriculum and Assessment Authority for Wales (Awdurdod Cwricwlwm Ac Asesu Cymru); the Scottish Consultative Council on the Curriculum; and the Northern Ireland Council for the Curriculum Examinations and Assessment.

Guidance and good practice

The national guidelines produced in England, Northern Ireland, Scotland and Wales are all referred to and a detailed breakdown of the requirements are listed. There is considerable common ground and care has been taken that no activity or suggestion would be invalid in any early years setting in the United Kingdom.

Personal, Social and Emotional Development is one of the most important areas of learning because it provides the underpinning skills which enable children to learn everything else offered to them. It would be wrong to make prescriptive recommendations for implementing the guidelines. The ideas in this book are designed to stimulate the imagination of the experienced teacher looking for new ideas or the novice in need of practical guidance.

Routines and activities

All the activities should be considered as merging into the normal life of the early years setting. The book stresses the importance of play and how the areas of learning are linked. The activities should not be seen as tasks to complete. They are designed to be manageable and fun. You may want to adapt and change them to make them more appropriate for the group of children you are teaching.

There are suggestions for 15 activities. Some are simple and straightforward which need few resources. Others are deliberately more challenging. They are planned to cover all aspects of personal, social and emotional development in the early years.

Some of your daily routines will foster Personal, Social and Emotional Development. Two of these, circle time and choosing time, have been looked at in detail with suggestions for new ideas to make the most of these activities. Some of your everyday equipment, such as home corners, specifically promote Personal, Social and Emotional Development. New ideas and a fresh look at this provision is included. Social skills that young children can find hard to master, such as sharing and waiting, are investigated. Areas that are awkward to teach or prove that you have covered are dealt with by offering broad-based games and ideas that you can play regularly. Common themes such as Seasons, Water, Colour, All about me and People who help us are covered and suggestions offered to include specific Personal, Social and Emotional Development targets in the planning stages of the process.

Ages and stages

Extension activities for older or more able children and methods for including younger children are suggested where appropriate. It is always difficult to pitch an activity at an exact stage and is probably less than useful to try. Part of the aim of Personal, Social and Emotional Development is to teach children to work together in groups. Young children should be encouraged to have a go and older children should be encouraged to investigate further. This is simply good practice. There are so many different stages of emotional development that you will spend much of your time initially observing, assessing and dealing with individual problems and weaknesses, without needing to set entire activities at any one stage.

Observing and assessing

There is no foolproof way to test that the provision you have made for the personal, social and emotional needs of the children in your care is working. Following good practice guidelines and working with the Early Learning Goals as a minimum curriculum requirement will start you off, but measuring emotional and social skills is, by nature, a negative exercise. You can quickly tell if a child is behaving inappropriately or if she has trouble expressing herself or if she is withdrawn and sad. Finding out how to provide an experience that will move the child nearer to the target is a difficult task.

Educational and developmental psychology are both subjects which require a great deal of specialist study, and to be considered experienced and qualified as a psychologist, able to judge specific behaviours and prescribe solutions for specific problems is not in the remit of the average early years practitioner. There is, therefore, a band of normality which we consider acceptable and children whose behaviour is consistently outside that band will, eventually, be referred for specialist help. In the meantime, your job is to offer experiences which will encourage children to grow in spirit.

Any form of assessment will be cumbersome and broad-based but it should be an indicator, a guide to possible problems.

The key to good provision is in the staff that deliver it. Researching best practice, keeping up-to-date with what others are doing and ongoing training designed to meet weak points is crucial.

Planning

A planning chart has been included for support and guidance but we would encourage you to adapt this readily to meet your own needs and circumstances.

There are seven books in this series, and although each book can be used by itself, they are designed to fit together so that the whole learning framework is covered.

The seven titles are:

❑ Personal, Social and Emotional Development

❑ Communication, Language and Literacy

❑ Mathematical Development

❑ Knowledge and Understanding of the World: Geography and History

❑ Knowledge and Understanding of the World: Science and Technology

❑ Physical Development

❑ Creative Development

All of these books carry some activities based on common themes which, when used together, will give enough ideas for a cross-curricular topic over a half or even a full term.

The common themes are:

❑ Seasons

❑ Water

❑ Colour

❑ All about me

❑ People who help us

All the books together provide an outline of the learning which should be taking place in the Foundation Stage.

Assessment

Each activity includes suggestions for assessment. Assessment involves two distinct activities:

❑ The gathering of information about the child's capabilities.

❑ Making a judgement based on this information.

Assessment should not take place in isolation. We assess to meet individual needs and ensure progress. The following ideas may help your assessment to be more effective.

❑ Assessment is a continuous process. It should be systematic to ensure all children are observed on a regular basis.

❑ Assessment should always start with the child. The first steps in providing appropriate provision is by sensitively observing children to identify their learning needs.

❑ Assessment should not take place to see how much the child has learned but to plan appropriately for future activities.

❑ You should be a participant in the assessment process, interacting and communicating with the child.

The main way of assessing the young child is through careful observation.

Observations should:

❑ Record both the positive and negative behaviour shown.

❑ Be long enough to make the child's behaviour meaningful.

❑ Record only what you see and not what you think you have seen or heard.

❑ Be clear - before you begin be sure you know what you want to observe.

❑ Be organised - plan ahead, otherwise it will not happen.

National guidelines

In Personal, Social and Emotional Development, the goals, guidance, desirable outcomes or framework (depending on where you live) are, not surprisingly, broadly similar. They may use different words, or the same words in a different order, but the intended outcome is the same – a sociable, happy, enquiring, confident, stimulated child who can communicate her needs, understand those of others and who is ready to move on and make the most of what school and life have to offer.

Legislating for such ethereal aims is difficult. Personal, Social and Emotional Development is the base on which all other learning is built and

therefore inextricably linked to all the other areas. This point is stressed in all of the curriculum guidelines. Having a series of aims can help to focus the mind of the practitioner whose job it is to plan ahead. However, no suggestion has been made that these are exhaustive lists for 'teaching by numbers'. They are there to guide, to stimulate and to suggest and are, in many opinions, a basic minimum requirement for the provision of adequate pre-school experience.

Common ground

There are different guidelines for practitioners in Wales, Scotland, Northern Ireland and England but, as you will see, the similarities far outweigh the differences.

A close look at the individual requirements shows that there is a vast amount of common ground.

Finding that common ground presents us with a useful indication of what is required across the board. Generally speaking, all the guidelines contain goals to encourage a child to acquire;

❑ Self-confidence

❑ Independence

❑ Understanding and acceptance of others beliefs

❑ Awareness of

the emotional and physical needs of others

❑ Appropriate expression of feelings

❑ Ability to relate to others

❑ Readiness to learn

The Scottish Curriculum Framework

'The importance of emotional, personal and social development cannot be over-emphasised', states the document.

Children should learn to:

❑ Develop confidence, self-esteem and a sense of security;

❑ Care for themselves and their personal safety;

❑ Develop independence, for example in dressing and personal hygiene;

❑ Persevere in tasks which at first present some difficulties;

❑ Express appropriately feelings, needs and preferences;

❑ Form positive relationships with other children and adults and begin to develop particular friendships with other children;

❑ Become aware of and respect the needs and feelings of others in their behaviour, and learn to follow rules;

❑ Make and express choices, plans and decisions;

❑ Play cooperatively, take turns and share resources;

❑ Become aware that the celebration of cultural and religious festivals is important in people's lives;

❑ Develop positive attitudes towards others whose gender, language, religion or culture, for example, is different from their own;

❑ Care for the environment and for other people in the community.

The Northern Ireland Curricular Guidance for Pre-School Education

The Northern Ireland guidance describes 'the characteristics and skills that the majority of children who have experienced appropriate pre-school education will display.' These are that:

❑ Children have a sense of personal worth;

❑ They show increasing self-confidence, self-control and self-discipline;

❑ They enjoy relationships with adults and other children and can work both independently or as part of a group;

❑ They are learning to share, take turns, follow and lead;

❑ They are becoming more sensitive to the needs and feelings of others;

❑ They demonstrate consideration for others by caring for and helping one another;

❑ They have some understanding of rules and routines and engage in acceptable behaviour;

❑ Children show some independence in dressing and in personal hygiene;

❑ They are eager to explore new learning;

❑ They persevere with tasks and seek help when needed and take pleasure in their achievements;

❑ They are learning to treat living things and the environment with respect, care and concern.

The Welsh Desirable Outcomes for Children's Learning before Compulsory School Age

'Children of nursery age will be learning about themselves' says the guidance. 'They will be learning about relationships … responsibilities … the world outside the family … and standards of good behaviour and developing appropriate attitudes.'

'It is not a self-contained checklist against which children can be tidily matched'.

Children should learn to:

❑ Feel confident and be able to form relationships with other children and with adults;

❑ Demonstrate care, respect and affection for other children and adults;

❑ Begin to show sensitivity to others and to those with difficulties;

❑ Concentrate for lengthening periods when involved in appropriate tasks;

❑ Explore and experiment confidently with new learning opportunities;

❑ Acknowledge the need for help and

seek help when needed;

❑ Begin to take responsibility for personal hygiene;

❑ Dress themselves, if given time and encouragement;

❑ Take turns, share and begin to exercise self-control;

❑ Understand that all living things should be treated with care, respect and concern;

❑ Respond positively to a range of new cultural and linguistic experiences.

The English Early Learning Goals

The document states: 'Successful personal, social and emotional development is critical for very young children in all aspects of their lives. It is also a pre-requisite for their success in all other areas of learning.'

Children should learn to:

❑ Be confident to try new activities, initiate ideas and speak in a familiar group;

❑ Form good relationships with adults and peers;

❑ Understand that they can expect others to treat their own needs, views, cultures and beliefs with respect;

❑ Work as part of a group or class, taking turns and sharing fairly, understanding that there needs to be agreed values and codes of behaviour for groups of people, including adults and children, to work together harmoniously;

❑ Continue to be interested, excited and motivated to learn;

❑ Select and use activities and resources independently;

❑ Dress and undress independently and manage their own personal hygiene;

❑ Have a developing awareness of their own needs, views and feelings and be sensitive to the needs, views and feelings of others;

❑ Have a developing respect for their own cultures and beliefs and those of other people;

❑ Understand that people have different needs, views, cultures and beliefs, which need to be treated with respect;

❑ Understand what is right, what is wrong and why;

❑ Consider the consequences of words and actions for themselves and others;

❑ Respond to significant experiences

showing a range of feelings when appropriate;

❑ Maintain attention, concentrate and sit quietly when appropriate.

Stepping stones

To help practitioners in planning, the English guidance identifies stepping stones that show 'the knowledge, skills, understanding and attitudes that children need to learn during the Foundation Stage in order to achieve the Early Learning Goals'. The Early Learning Goals form the final stepping

stones. Adding stepping stones to the guidelines allows groups to monitor progress towards a goal. This is a key factor in the usefulness of the information that you are collecting about each child as they progress. The stepping stones carefully avoid the use of age as a marker, preferring to allow for the different stages to be reached in the child's own time.

Good early years practitioners understand that children have to work

towards a goal before they achieve it and will automatically be putting into practice this staged approach. Allowing for differences in achievement is important in the creation of individual learning plans. You need to know where on a scale a child is before you can help her move on. Recording how and when each child reaches each stepping stone on the way towards the final goal is a useful indication of the ease with which the child has learned.

Planning to meet the guidelines

These guidelines alone are not enough. How you plan your curriculum must also take into account the culture and policy of the group and make the most of every opportunity.

No child will be taught to be kind to others through a series of planned activities. She will learn by example from the adults that are kind to her.

How you present experiences and how you interact with children, their parents, other adults and each other is as crucial as any of the goals themselves.

The English Early Learning Goals document suggests that to give all children the best opportunities for Personal, Social and Emotional Development, practitioners should plan for:

❑ Activities that promote emotional, moral, spiritual and social development alongside intellectual development;

❑ Experiences that help children develop autonomy and the disposition to learn;

❑ Opportunities to give positive encouragement to children with practitioners acting as positive role models;

❑ Positive images in, for example, books and displays that challenge children's thinking;

❑ Opportunities for children to work alone and in small and large groups;

❑ Activities which are imaginative and enjoyable;

❑ The development of independence skills in those children who are highly dependent upon adult support for personal care;

❑ Support and a structured approach to achieve the successful social and emotional development of vulnerable children and those with particular behavioural difficulties, including those with autistic spectrum disorders;

❑ Opportunities for play and learning that take account of children's particular religious and cultural beliefs;

❑ Constructive relationships between children and practitioners, practitioners and children and with parents and workers from other agencies;

❑ Opportunities to observe, assess and plan the next stage in children's learning;

❑ Relevant training to improve practitioner's knowledge, skills and understanding.

Assessing your own achievements, the balance of your curriculum and the effectiveness of the activities on offer is just as important as assessing the children who are in your group. Planning ahead is the key to ensuring that you cover all the goals at all the stages with all of the children!

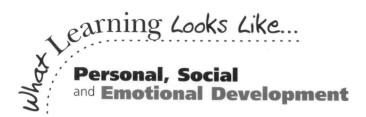

Personal, Social and Emotional Development

The area of learning explained

Personality, high self-esteem and the ability to cope with life are all part of what many parents would put at the top of their wish list for their children. Often they choose just one word – happiness. Generally speaking, happy adults are motivated and balanced, friendly, confident, capable and able to socialise and maintain positive relationships of all kinds. Starting the ball rolling in the right direction is the essence of supporting personal, social and emotional development in young children.

Prescribed outcomes or goals in personal, emotional and social development can only ever be short-term guidelines. There is no finite term during which we learn how to be adult and mature. Any person of any age, if prepared to answer honestly, would admit that they are trying to change an attitude or develop a strength in one area or another.

The first steps

No child joins a group as a blank page. Many would argue that no child is even born a blank page. Genetics, experience *in utero* and even birth itself are all believed to influence the adult we will eventually become. The first few days of life, the shock of light, noise, touch and taste and the child's experiences of these new stimuli form the first steps in their personal, social and emotional development. The parent's response to their child's crying is the first interaction. Within just a few days of birth, the child has experienced many emotions from pain and fear to pleasure and relief.

By six weeks this tiny baby is quite an expert. By the time she can physically smile, she is ready to use that smile to elicit responses from others around her. This is an advanced skill and one which many adults would benefit from remembering! If at this stage the child is not reliably rewarded, if only by another smile in response, the value of smiling as a social tool may become, for that person, lessened. If this baby expects her basic needs to be met and her world to be safe, she is then free to fine-tune her emotional and social skills as she grows up.

Babies who babble at an adult and get a response will learn that talking is a useful communication tool and are ready to learn how to express themselves. Babies whose first games are treated with respect and humour will learn that social interaction is an enriching and appealing activity. Finger games, lullabies, clapping games, bubble blowing and bath-time play are invaluable for all aspects of learning. Even peek-a-boo teaches object permanence, interactive humour, hand-eye coordination and early language skills! This is the real beginning of emotional well-being.

Many of the children who join a pre-school group are safe, nurtured, loved and supported and are ready for the next step. Some, however, are not. It is the recognition of the stage and level

of readiness of each individual child that makes the difference between good early years provision and provision which is patchy and off-balanced. There can be many reasons why a child has not reached readiness yet. Some disabilities delay development, some home environments are more enriching than others and being aware of the effects of neglect and abuse is a valuable first step in recognising which children need extra support.

What do we want?

What do we want from our Personal, Social and Emotional Development curriculum? Times change, demands on children change as quickly and keeping in touch with what is required is difficult.

How many times have you heard the phrase, 'It wasn't like that in my day' (meaning 'and I'm OK'!)? Not so long ago children were being taught:

❑ That silence is golden;

❑ To be seen and not heard;

❑ Not to speak unless they were spoken to;

❑ That mothers knew best.

Now we want children to be:

❑ Sociable;

❑ Popular;

❑ Kind;

❑ Communicative;

❑ Intelligent;

❑ Creative;

❑ Happy and settled;

❑ Innovative and enquiring.

Linking personal development, emotional development and social development in one heading is useful in terms of setting broad categories, but in reality there are many different

requirements for each area. If you add the differing requirements of each culture, sub-group and then family to the equation, the list of behaviours to deal with is endless. Understanding which behaviour is generally covered by which area may help to provide a more balanced early years experience.

Emotional development

Emotions colour our lives, whether it be fear, joy, anxiety, pleasure, anticipation, sadness, anger, sympathy, passion, relief, love, hate, shame, disgust or surprise. Being in touch with our feelings and trusting them enough to be able to express them helps us to move forward, heal emotional wounds and learn about our real selves as we grow up.

Negative emotions are part of life. Learning to name them is perhaps the first stage in accepting that they exist. Fairy stories are often scary and modern day classics incorporate frightening ideas on purpose: children need to learn to manage fear. They need to know that they can be afraid and still be all right. Not being afraid of fear and using our past experiences as learning tools is a big step on the road to maturity. Expecting to be able to cope, not being overwhelmed and powerless is part of that learning process, too, and one which early years professionals can actively teach young children.

Positive emotions such as pleasure, love, relief and joy are the rewards we search for throughout most of our lives. Experiencing positive emotions is an invaluable gift that we as adults can bestow on the next generations. In your setting, you can plan for the children in your care to expect to feel good about their experiences with you. Good early years experiences teach children to expect success, measurable in terms of positive emotions. Naming these emotions and recognising how you got them is how you learn to do it again.

Social development

In today's multicultural society and with values changing from decade to decade, being socially adept and

Personal development

There are whole companies of trainers, therapists, authors, consultants and self-help groups whose sole purpose is to support adult personal development. If comparing the angst of adulthood with the development needs of children seems at first inappropriate, look again at the theme that runs through the personal development industry – find yourself, understand your own needs, find fulfilment and identify the meaning in your own life. All these aims are admirable, indeed enviable, and relate to one basic need - happiness.

To be happy, we need to know what we want. Knowing what we want out of a changing and confusing life relies on us knowing who we are and what we like. Self-esteem allows us to consider this as important. In fact, it is essential.

Self-esteem protects us from other people's opinions. Self-esteem allows us to express ourselves, change situations, embrace success and learn from failure. It is the rod that keeps our chins up when life is hard. Self-esteem allows us to hear the knocking of opportunity. It is the bag in which we carry our personality. Without self-esteem, we are walking in the dark. Teaching it is, unfortunately, impossible. The baby that was left too long to cry, unfed and unloved; the toddler whose games were ignored and the child who never speaks out all have steeper hills to climb than they should have.

Early years settings have a responsibility to the whole child and that includes the child's family. Some children may need professional help, others no more than someone to be proud of them. Praise goes a long way in the nurturing of self-esteem and consequent success. Success is essential and it is the job of any group to ensure that young children experience success as often as possible.

A way of life

Personal, social and emotional development is not supported by following steps to a goal or objective - it is an ethos, a way of life, a culture of support. Nurturing it is about evaluating every one of your dealings with the child or family in terms of its positive or negative reinforcement. How you plan your day, your equal opportunities policy, your understanding of each child's needs, the physical environment you create, the staff you employ, the books you choose, the games you play, the activities you offer, the behaviour you praise, the behaviour you condemn - this is what Personal, Social and Emotional Development is all about.

socially acceptable is not clearly defined. The essence of social development is being able to recognise what is expected from you in which situation, evaluating that information and making a decision about your own behaviour based on experience and an understanding of what is going on around you. Your role is to make clear what the rules are in known environments, such as home and nursery, and that the rules can differ without either being wrong.

Manipulating social situations, predicting responses, eliciting attention and instigating change are social skills that babies learn quickly. Children starting nursery come with a veritable armoury of social weaponry. How you accommodate them will have a great bearing on how they accommodate your requirements later on. How you behave towards the children will have a direct and immediate effect on their social success.

What you praise and reward gives clear messages about your value system. Are children praised for being quiet and unobtrusive or for asking pertinent questions? If a child changes the activity she is doing to suit some personal investigation, is she being disruptive or enquiring? When did you last praise a child for telling a good joke (even if you have heard it hundreds of times before!)? How up-to-date are you on anger management? Does your practice really match your equal opportunities policy?

Equal opportunities

No child should feel less worthy than another. Your aim should be to help raise a generation that accepts differences in others and allows people to be judged on personal merit and not cultural or gender issues. This is at the heart of emotional maturity and social development. Children need to know about others in order to allay the fears and misconceptions that

ignorance brings. Children who feel isolated and inferior will have emotional baggage that will hinder them as adults. Understanding what equal opportunities really means and the investment of skill and time in the introduction of an active policy are essential if you intend to support Personal, Social and Emotional Development in every child. It is not just the children who feel second best that are suffering; the ones who feel superior are just as likely to encounter problems in the adult world.

Gender issues are still widely misunderstood. Girls do not have to be like boys or boys like girls. Girls should be like themselves and feel valued. Boys should be like themselves and feel valued. Boys should respect girls and girls should respect boys. Social development depends on it. Boys deserve to be allowed to explore their emotions whilst not sacrificing the positive essence of their masculinity.

Elements of school readiness

Confidence: A sense of control and mastery of one's body, behaviour and world; the child's sense that he is more likely than not to succeed at what he undertakes, and that adults will be helpful.

Curiosity: The sense that finding out about things is positive and leads to pleasure.

Intentionality: The wish and capacity to have an impact, and to act upon that with persistence. This is related to a sense of competence, of being effective.

Self-control: The ability to modulate and control one's own actions in age-appropriate ways; a sense of inner control.

Relatedness: The ability to engage with others based on the sense of being understood by and understanding others.

Capacity to communicate: The wish and ability to verbally exchange ideas, feelings and concepts with others, including adults.

Cooperativeness: The ability to balance one's own needs with those of others in group activity.

(from Daniel Goleman's book, *Emotional Intelligence*)

place can the human mind hope to reach personal or academic potential.

Managing an early years curriculum with Personal, Social and Emotional Development in mind should begin to affect the quality and success of all other goals. Working with children who are age-appropriately mature, capable and keen makes for a different environment than working with troubled or unnecessarily difficult children.

Sharing information

Passing information from one setting to the next is crucial to the accurate assessment of each child's progress through the Foundation Stage. It is up to individual groups to manage this crucial transition. Keeping records of the assessments you have carried out as the child passes through each stage is an important part of the links needed between early years and Key Stage 1 environments.

Some children will not reach the same stage as their peers. This will indicate to the school that there is a potential problem. If adequate information is passed on to the school the valuable time that is often lost while reception teachers reach the same conclusion that nursery teachers have already reached will be gained.

Other children will streak ahead and be trying out quite difficult concepts before they start school. Settings which have policies for stretching able children will be able to keep the enthusiasm of the able child going.

In the field of Personal, Social and Emotional Development the boundaries are a little blurred at the best of times and assessing progress will always be a thorny problem. 'Age and stage' assessment must, however, be done and although it cannot be the

Equal opportunites for disabled people does not mean a toilet with a wide door. Accepting disability is an issue for all of us, not just the disabled. I recently tried to take a disabled child swimming and rang in advance. Did the pool have disabled facilities? Yes? Good! What hoist was there to get the child into the pool? None? Oh! What facilities do you have then? A changing room set aside. What was in the changing room - a bench or supportive seat? No. Oh. How do your other disabled clients get into the water? They walk. Oh. What was that pool manager's idea of disability? I wonder.

How many children are stuck in isolation because they cannot physically get out? What about their social and emotional development? How must it feel to be persistently excluded from everyday activities? What good are we doing our able-bodied children by protecting them from the reality of disability? Why do so few picture books show disabled children doing ordinary things? Partly because it is still difficult for them to be involved in ordinary

things and partly because they do not yet enter our collective thoughts. Personal development is not just about accepting one's own disabilities but about accepting disability in others, too. The resources are not widely available for you easily to do justice to this important subject yet but with imagination and compassion you can teach acceptance and appropriate inclusion in your groups.

Emotional intelligence

Daniel Goleman, in his book *Emotional Intelligence* (Bloomsbury Press), argues that it can matter more than IQ. He identifies crucial 'windows of opportunity' when physiological development and emotional development allow a child to be receptive to 'emotional coaching'. The idea that emotional intelligence can be learned and relearned and that there are specific periods of receptivity adds weight to the argument that early years education should be primarily about the fostering and support of such skill. Only when these basic systems are in whole picture of a child's personality it can be a guide to potential problems.

Assessing progress in Personal, Social and Emotional Development

Assessing whether or not a child has reached a specific goal in Personal, Social and Emotional Development is hard to measure. Observing a child at play and during the day is the only appropriate method - testing is not an option. An understanding of the goal itself and what it means in terms of behaviour is crucial and the staff team will need to be well aware of what is expected by the goals, what is expected by the group and what the individual curriculum is offering the child in terms of supportive experience.

When assessing Personal, Social and Emotional Development, keep in mind that the aim is a sociable, happy and functioning child who is able to grow emotionally, making the most of what is on offer. If that is what you see as you observe the child in different situations then you will find that the boxes are all automatically ticked! If not, your job is to identify the problems, the causes and the solutions.

The 'tick box' culture that most early years professionals have fought against is becoming almost inevitable. The complicated systems that are in place to allow flexibility alongside accountability are still a system of boxes to be ticked. That we are now working within this system does not mean that we cannot still fully develop the ideas and creative play

experiences that we have always found to be most beneficial to the children. Remember, have the idea first and then find the box that it best fits in and not the other way round! Use the boxes to suggest areas that you have not yet covered and concentrate on those for a while but take care not to limit your own ideas to the boxes that require ticks.

The activities suggested in this book are linked to relevant Early Learning Goals. Pointers to look out for during assessment sessions are given for each activity. Record what you see happening and wait until you have a full set of observations before attempting to create a bigger picture. You will have to allow for a child having an off day before you record that the child is unable to relate to his or her peers. It is unreasonable to

suggest that because a child does not play well with one of her peers she has a social problem. She may not like that child! Being reasonable and realistic is the key to successful observations. Taking frequent and regular observations of a child in different situations is the best way to build up a true picture of that child's stage of personal, social and emotional development. Be alerted by one-off occurrences by all means but allow yourself to be reassured that some behaviour really is a one-off. Children learn by having experienced rejection of this bad behaviour and you could find that you present an inaccurate picture of a child if you judge him or her on too small a sample of behaviour. This approach is important across the curriculum but clearly it is crucial when assessing Personal, Social and Emotional Development.

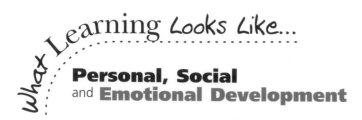

Links with other areas of learning

It is possible to include activities in your day which support Personal, Social and Emotional Development but at very best they can only be an indicator of your success in all the other areas of the curriculum. As a reminder to staff about good practice, they are invaluable, and to help you to focus assessment on particular children on a particular day in a particular situation they may be useful, too. As discussion starting points, as introduction to new vocabulary, as the opportunity to sow the seeds of an idea, these activities are well worth the time and effort, but if the intention is to teach to a goal, then any one-off activity will fail.

Greater success is possible through a look at the daily routine:

❑ Is it a nurturing environment?

❑ Do children have time to finish projects?

❑ Are they praised enough?

❑ Do they have time to chat to each other?

❑ Do they have time to chat to you?

❑ Do you have regular circle times?

❑ How well do you really know the parents of the children in your group?

❑ Are your observations of individual children coming up with any issues that indicate your curriculum might not be supporting social development?

❑ How do you use your home corner?

❑ How supported and positive do your staff feel?

❑ Above all, is it fun being in your group?

Measuring ability in personal, social and emotional development terms is also difficult. There are always children in a group who do not get on with the others or who are unhappy or who bully. Working on problems seems to be the rather negative way we deal with this. Prevention being better than cure, we perhaps need to be looking at all our children, specifically to assess their stage of personal, social and emotional development, setting targets and working towards those targets.

Imagine that a child, Jake, is unpopular. No-one wants to sit next to him. You ask Laura to sit next to him. She complains, so you tell her to be kind to Jake and sit down. Laura explains to you that she is afraid because Jake always pinches the person he is sitting next to.

The basic problem is that having Jake sit next to you when you are doing something interesting is not a positive experience. Any child would be forgiven for wriggling away, further alienating and angering him - and so the spiral continues.

If you were to: notice the problem, recognise what was happening, teach Jake not to pinch, and then follow up with positive reinforcement by encouraging others to sit next to him,

safely, you would have dealt with the issue effectively. You would have taught Jake more sociable behaviour, reinforced his neighbours' right not to be pinched and you would have become more aware that there are patterns of behaviour that Jake may need further help with.

You should praise Laura for her confidence in speaking out and assure her that you have taken what she said seriously. You would also have made the learning experience that you were hoping to deliver at that activity table accessible to more children and with a higher likely success rate.

There are different stages of Personal, Social and Emotional Development, just as there are in all areas. One of the worst insults a pre-school child can say to another is 'Baby!'. Children who are not fitting in, who are not behaving in an age appropriate manner and who are, indeed, behaving like a much younger child, will need help to catch up with their peers. Recognising problems in this area will pave the way for greater enjoyment of and success in all areas of the curriculum.

Communication, Language and Literacy

We give others great insight into our inner selves when we talk. If children have positive experiences of early communication, they are more likely to want to continue and go on to enjoy reading and writing. If they mistrust themselves as communicators and are afraid of the insights that communication gives others, they may well resist learning language.

Enjoyment of a wide variety of experiences is valuable in the formation of vocabulary and expressive skills. If children have limited understanding of their own lives and if they have not been supported in their exploration of that world, reading becomes harder.

Books allow us to explore a wider world. Stories help us deal with some of our worst fears and greatest passions. Drama and poetry allow us to consider the idea that there is often more than one way of doing something and story corners are wonderful places to cuddle up in.

Mathematical Development

Having control over what at first glance seems chaotic is a reassuring feeling. Experiencing measurable success is strengthening. Being right is also good fun. It is easy to be right in early years maths. Two and two are four and that is that. Beginning to realise that some elements of the world can be ordered and predictable is a good feeling. If a child needs praise, then maths is the first place to start: 'Can you pass me one brick, Emma?' 'Well done!'

Knowledge and Understanding of the World

Understanding heralds acceptance and reduces fear. Understanding how shadows work, for example, will calm a fearful child at night. Explaining thunder will turn a frightening noise into a fascinating occurrence in the child's eyes.

Intellectual exploration is a brand new concept to the pre-school child and is a source of wonder and excitement as the world outside the family begins to open up. To foster that sense of wonder and interest and to make the knowledge accessible and interesting is the first and most important step in teaching a child how to learn. There are countless topics and subjects that fascinate young children. The sheer

number of questions one small child can ask in a day is testament to this fact and to use these questions as your starting point is a wonderful way of harnessing some of the intellectual energy that children in this age group are just discovering. However, the flexibility, experience and up-to-date knowledge that this requires is no small matter. Teach a child how to find out by looking things up yourself. We are all regularly asked questions to which we do not know the answer.

Physical Development

Taking risks and being brave are essential aspects of Personal, Social and Emotional Development. The sense of achievement that a child gets by conquering a hill, jumping off something that seems high and being praised for 'having a go' are as important as the physical dexterity they are developing at the same time. Knowing that one's body will do surprising things if asked to comes as quite a surprise to many people and is usually a pleasant discovery.

Children who are afraid of risks and who are rendered helpless by the fear of tripping up are missing out on a good feeling. Physical success is a great boost to morale and one which is relatively easy to provide. Meeting the child at the stage they are at and moving on from there will enable you both to reap rewards. Communication, expression and sociability are all boosted when a child feels brave and proud of an achievement. Conquering fear is important. Understanding the level of risk involved in an activity, judging if the feeling of success is worth that risk and either suffering the consequences or enjoying the glory are valuable life lessons.

Being brave when tired, hot and maybe even a little bruised, is good for personal pride. Socially it is a boon, too - children are quick to mock a cry baby and no-one enjoys the company

of a moaning Minnie. There is a balance between bravery and common sense and finding that balance enables a child to benefit from the physical activities on offer.

Personal safety is a great reassurance. If you know that your safety is in your hands then you can tackle more interesting and challenging obstacles. If you are learning how to judge risk and keep yourself safe now, when you are older and more capable, you have a reservoir of experience to help you decide how to manage potentially dangerous situations.

Creative Development

Many therapists choose art and creative activities as a tool for healing emotional wounds. This basic form of expression is an intensely personal statement.

'You'll have to do that again, houses don't have pink and purple windows', a teacher once said to a five-year-old. 'How can I put that on the wall?'

Creativity is the beginning of real personality. Expression of emotions that you don't have the vocabulary for (especially as a young child) is a cathartic experience that requires concentration, being left to get on with it and definitely no judgment on the result. 'Can you tell me about your picture?' is a useful opener if you need one. Then listen.

Modelling, music, dance, painting and drawing all provide a creative outlet that is a personal development tool *par excellence*. Children play hard, they create stories and colours, monsters and angels with paint, old curtains, percussion instruments and a free-ranging imagination that too many so-called educational experiences sadly stamp out. Education means, literally, 'to lead out'. Bringing out the potential in a child is most rewarding in the field of creativity.

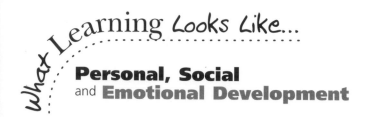

The importance of play

Play is absolutely essential but it is often misunderstood and maligned. No goals or guidelines will ever be able to capture the possibilities offered to a child who is allowed to play. Because many adults have forgotten how to play and cannot fully understand the activity, it has lost its popularity and we have opted for something easier to measure.

The power of play

Dr Benjamin Spock said on play with babies: 'When you hug him or make noises at him, when you show him that you think he's the most wonderful baby in the world, it makes his spirit grow, just the way milk makes his bones grow.'

Penelope Leach, in *Children First*, explains that 'through self-motivated play and endless talk they [children] must incorporate the puzzlements of themselves, other people, feelings, processes and objects into a constructed reality which they can share with adults. Early childhood education can help them do all that; help them towards the shared reality and the dawning ability to think about it conceptually that will mark their first readiness for school and lessons – and the five to seven shift. What it cannot and should not seek to do is hurry children through these necessary

processes of growth and maturation. Good early childhood education has its own validity. "Pre-school" may describe its time frame but it does not describe its purpose.'

Learning through play

The Scottish Curriculum Framework makes an attempt to bring play back into the frame with its suggestion that 'play makes a powerful contribution to children's learning. It provides opportunities for children to:

❑ make sense of real life situations;

❑ develop awareness of themselves and others;

❑ explore, investigate and experiment;

❑ be actively involved in learning;

❑ draw and test their conclusions;

❑ express their ideas and feelings in many different ways;

❑ inhabit imagined situations;

❑ act out and come to terms with experiences at home or with friends;

❑ be solitary, quiet and reflective;

❑ collaborate with others;

❑ take the initiative on their own terms;

❑ develop relationships;

❑ practise skills;

❑ consolidate previous learning;

❑ be challenged in new learning.'

What you offer makes a difference to the standard of the provision but play is the backbone. The basic tools of play begin to teach young children the first stages of life lessons that few adults can honestly say they have completely mastered.

❑ Home corner – how to behave in situations, how to make sense of new environments.

❑ Dressing up – how it feels to be someone else, how others might see you.

❑ Role play and make believe – imagining new situations and facing the fearful dragons that lurk around the corner before you have to in reality.

❑ Stories – how to communicate, how others have made sense of the world, what others think, situations that others have been in, new ideas, new concepts, a window onto the outside world from the safety of a secure place.

❑ Sand and water trays – how things work, how to investigate, how to describe, how to cooperate.

❑ Puppets and drama – communicating and empathising, creativity, design, expression, stories in three dimensions.

❑ Arts and crafts – expression, solitary absorption in one activity, concentration, imagination, creativity.

The stages of play

There are different stages in play. First, the child will play entirely alone, absorbed in investigating an object and finding out as much as possible about it - visualise an eight-month-old with a bunch of keys.

The next stage is when a child will play alongside another child, constantly looking over to see what the other is doing but still immersed in a private world of her own. Imagine two toddlers at a group, each sitting at their parents' feet and each building their own tower.

Then, before the child joins a group of children of her own age, she

becomes ready for interactive play. It is the play of cooperation - 'I'll be the driver and you can be the passenger, yeah?'

Each stage branches out into different types of play and at each stage the role of adults is different. Baby play is about learning to trust and communicate; toddler play is about learning how different objects behave; interactive play is about combining these skills to move into the world of imaginative and constructive interactions with other people.

Adult involvement

It's a shame that so many adults have forgotten how to play. How much easier it would be if you could just get down and play, using your adult knowledge to guide the game and yet keep the freshness and vitality of the world through the child's eyes!

The attitude of the adults who care for children is the prime factor in the success of any provision. Energy, enthusiasm, interest, sensitivity, humour and imagination make such a difference. Adults who can really play make the best teachers and, often, the happiest people.

Success and failure in play situations

Some cultures, notably the Chinese, do not readily accept the notion of failure. They see failure as a new opportunity for a different success. The Chinese word for failure means opportunity. Remembering this when we cannot immediately see the benefit of yet another failure is the basis of optimism and an ability to persevere. Persevering when failure strikes is a personal skill that has been responsible for many of the greatest scientific discoveries and artistic careers in history.

Teaching children to learn that 'failure' means 'not having success yet' and to think laterally to solve problems is a great gift. Being able to solve problems on a day-to-day basis makes life much easier, it is as simple as that. Giving up the first time a brick tower collapses is a waste of a good opportunity to learn not just about building towers, shapes and motor control, but about perseverance as well. Encourage your children to stop and think of another way to try.

Personal, Social and **Emotional Development**

Circle time

Meeting the needs of a child's personal, social and emotional development curriculum is not done by offering specific activities now and again. It is achieved by making sure that the daily routines you practise offer a supportive and safe environment to nurture the child's growing self-confidence. Circle time, talk-about time, group time - whatever you call it - is where you practise what you preach.

In adult therapy, circle time is used in many counselling arenas. It offers a safe space for adults who have suffered abuse or addiction to talk about the issues they have faced in a non-threatening and supportive environment. The security is established by agreeing rules of behaviour within the group beforehand and by having a named leader who will maintain the smooth running of the session. As a behaviour management tool, circle time is used to help people who find controlling their behaviour challenging. The theory goes that practising social interaction in a supportive environment will encourage those for whom sociability is difficult to learn. Coming to difficult decisions is easier in a formal group where the responsibility

may be shared – many a committee is essentially a grown-up circle time session!

In secondary schools, circle time is still a preparation for the real business of grown-up decisions. Spiritual and moral dilemmas can be faced and understood in a circle time session. In junior schools, the children use the sessions to begin to express their feelings, what makes them feel good or bad and why. In infant schools, the children use circle time to practise the

sound of their own voice and to ensure that they understand the basic rules of communication, letting others speak and listening to others' opinions.

What, then, is expected of circle time in the early years setting? Expecting a child of three or four to be able to discuss and co-operate on the same level as an adult is plainly inappropriate.

Theory and research

Peter Lang of the Institute of Education at the University of Warwick argues that although circle time is becoming increasingly widespread in this country, it is unfocused in British schools compared to other countries.

That there is little theory underpinning the practice is an issue that we should be concerned about. His paper, *Getting Round to Clarity*, describes examples of the development of circle time in other countries - America, Scandinavia and Italy. Americans are offered guidance on the development of self-awareness at specific ages; Italians work in small groups to improve the teacher-pupil relationship and the child's self-esteem; and the Scandinavians have developed clear practice guidelines for all users of circle time.

Studying child development and knowing what is appropriate for each stage is a good place to begin an evaluation of current practice. Piaget's pre-operational stage (two to seven years) identifies the egocentricity of children of nursery age. Expecting an egocentric being to fully empathise with another person would, following Piaget's theory, be unrealistic. Thorndike and Skinner (child development psychologists famous for their work on conditioning - nature versus nurture)believed that the Law of Effect meant that if something good followed an action then the action would be repeated. This theory forms the basis for most behaviour modification plans and highlights the need for circle time to be a planned, positive and effective session.

All settings should, therefore, as a bare minimum, be able to evaluate the content of their circle time to ensure that the expectations of the group are achievable and the children are being effectively encouraged, at an age appropriate level, to become the social beings they are hoping for.

Learning what is right and wrong is an important part of the socialisation process. Circle time is one place where socialisation can be explored but the strongest influences surround the child at home and are rooted in her experiences of life in general. Simply including circle time in a timetable is no absolver of responsibility elsewhere in the curriculum. Feeling good enough to behave well is often a self-esteem issue.

The development of self-esteem has been studied in depth by Jenny Mosley, author of the books *Turn Your School Around* and *Quality Circle Time in the Primary Classroom.* Her model of circle time is to build the self-esteem of each participant and to encourage pupils to take responsibility for the consequences of their actions. Her model claims to impact in many areas of life such as individual motivation and achievement, enhancing positive relationships, personal and social development and producing calm behaviour and self-discipline. Early

Early Learning Goals

These activities will help you work towards the following goals:

❑ Be confident to try new activities, initiate ideas and speak in a familiar group.

❑ Form good relationships with adults and peers.

❑ Understand that they can expect others to treat their own needs, views, cultures and beliefs with respect.

❑ Work as part of a group or class, taking turns and sharing fairly, understanding that there needs to be agreed values and codes of behaviour for groups of people, including adults and children, to work together harmoniously.

❑ Continue to be interested, excited and motivated to learn.

❑ Have a developing awareness of their own needs, views and feelings and be sensitive to those of others.

❑ Understand what is right, what is wrong and why.

❑ Consider the consequences of words and actions for themselves and others.

❑ Maintain attention, concentrate and sit quietly when appropriate.

years practitioners will be able to take a great deal from the primary model so clearly presented by Jenny Mosley but must always remember that three- and four-year-olds are not the same as primary school children.

The early years are different. Nursery children are still learning to talk. Daring to speak out in a group is a major issue, never mind the content of the utterance. The conversational skills that the baby, toddler and pre-schooler have absorbed are only just proving useful. Your main responsibility is to build the child's ability to explore,

express and discuss later in life. You are building the foundations, not painting the roof! Your circle time will, therefore, be different.

The management of circle time

In the management of circle time, praising contributions and developing conversation are key issues. Conversation is quite different from talking. Encourage conversation throughout the day and train staff to listen to children and to praise verbal contributions.

Using trained staff is important - getting circle time wrong is worse than not doing it at all. You may encounter a child who discloses a serious personal issue to the group and the staff member must be able to manage such an event. Observations of children within this situation are a useful indication of the child's general development, too. Make the most of it and have an observer as well as a leader.

Verbal put-downs and unkindness damage young children. Setting up a space that you are calling safe to talk in makes you even more responsible for the safety of the child within that space. Circle time should, therefore, not be taken lightly or without research and training.

A great deal of the most effective work on early years self-esteem and confidence will be done outside circle time but, as a preparation for more formal discussion groups, circle time is a valuable curriculum tool and, used well, will be a benefit to all involved.

Calm and quiet

Plan for circle time and evaluate your success or failure as you would any other session. Circle time should be a relaxed session where everyone can join in and you can get to know the children in your care a little better. Your aim is to allow them the opportunity to get used to speaking out in a group and also to having their comments listened to with respect. You might use circle time as an opportunity to introduce new ideas or to go over old issues - either way it should be a reassuring time of calm and quiet.

Set the space up somewhere where you are unlikely to be disturbed. A carpeted area is ideal. Some groups have a formal circle with children and adults cross-legged around the perimeter. Others form a group, sitting on knees or cuddled in a corner. If you have a larger group with more than six or so children, then the informal cuddle corner may become hard to manage, but with fewer children it can be cosy and comforting. A group of more than 12 pre-school children is hard to manage effectively at circle time and you should consider breaking the class up into smaller groups for this special time of the day.

Children under the age of three are unlikely to benefit from circle time and will probably disrupt the group. New or shy children will probably want to sit on the leader's lap, which is fine for a while, but integrating them into the group and making sure that everyone gets their fair share of cuddles is important, too.

Rules and routine

Children of this age love routine. They like to know what is going to happen next and this applies as much to circle time as it does to any other session. You may find that starting with a story will put the children at ease and encourage them to contribute later on in the session. Try not to go over 20 minutes, as the children's attention span will not stretch further.

When you start your circle time, you will be aware of the themes and topics that the group is currently covering. Picking rhymes and games which

support new learning is a good idea, although being too rigid could lead to a stilted session. There are always some children who always want the same rhyme no matter what the theme. Accommodate them without boring everyone else by having that rhyme sometimes.

The introduction of new vocabulary is an important part of early years work and giving the children confidence to try new words is an appropriate and useful activity for circle time. Choose appropriate words that link with your theme and have a simple definition prepared beforehand. Try not to use new words in the definition or you will quickly confuse the children. Show pictures that may encourage comment or conversation and ask simply what the children think is happening or how the people in the picture feel (Sunday magazines are a good source of this type of photo, but filter them carefully).

The rules of your group may, to you, seem perfectly clear - the children may even understand them perfectly, but they will get broken nonetheless. Minor problems can usually be solved in a non-confrontational way if you gently remind the whole group that throwing sand or spitting or whatever the sin is that has been committed is not allowed and explain again why. Circle time is often used in schools to underline the rules and sanctions of the class. Your children are too young for you to dwell too heavily on this aspect of circle time but it is useful to raise points now and again. You can use this time for praising too – in fact, if you have had a minor moan then praising ought to follow pretty quickly!

Games and rhymes

There are plenty of games and rhymes that encourage the children to engage in question and answer sessions. Setting the scene for conversation this way will lead gently into a more general discussion time. If the child

has heard her own voice as part of a game, then speaking out an individual comment is slightly less frightening.

Rhymes to get attention or to signal the start of a session are useful in circle time as they are throughout the day. Start singing the first line and let it be a signal that the children should join in, and at the end they should be sitting quietly.

> Clapping hands can sound like rain
>
> Clap clap clap clap clap
>
> I turn around and clap again
>
> Clap clap clap clap clap
>
> Sitting down we clap our knees
>
> Clap clap clap clap clap
>
> Now we're sitting quite still please
>
> Clap clap clap clap clap

(to the tune of the first two lines of 'Old Macdonald' repeated)

Finger rhymes and games, even old favourites, can be given a new lease of life by changing the names used to the names of the children instead. 'Peter Pointer, Peter Pointer, Where are you?' can easily become 'Emma Smith, Emma Smith, Where are you?' and will encourage Emma to reply 'Here I am, Here I am, How do you do?'. Try choosing the quieter children; it will give them the opportunity to speak out in a safe and structured environment.

Ending the session with a short period of silence is a powerful tool. Sitting still and quietly and gathering one's thoughts before the next activity is a good way of learning concentration skills. But don't be too ambitious - one minute is a long time to be silent!

What to do if ...

The children don't settle

❑ Make sure that you are doing it at the right time of day, when the children are not too tired.

❑ Don't keep them waiting on the mat while you prepare yourself.

❑ Start with something more interesting.

A young child walks away

❑ Let them go. There will be other adults around who can occupy the child who is obviously not ready for this yet.

An older child walks away

❑ Have a spare adult sit with the child to encourage him or her to stay. Observe the child throughout the day and make sure that she is generally able to concentrate and join in. Failure to do so may indicate a problem.

A child disrupts the group by fidgeting and bothering the children around her

❑ Have a spare adult sit with that child. Work towards her being able to sit on her own.

More than one child regularly disrupts the group

❑ Make the time more interesting!

❑ Evaluate your own skills.

A child discloses a serious problem such as abuse

❑ Don't over-react.

❑ Make sure that the child has finished talking before you thank her for contributing.

❑ Don't ask probing questions.

❑ Finish the session.

❑ Find an excuse for someone to play one-to-one with the child while urgent expert advice is sought from the duty social worker.

A child gives you the same 'news' each day

This is very common. Praise the contribution and move on. After several sessions of repetition, you might like to help the child to say something else. Prompt them with a question, such as 'Didn't I see you going home for tea with Sam yesterday? What did you play with at Sam's house?' or whatever.

A child never contributes

❑ Prompt the child with a question and then praise any contribution.

❑ Monitor the child throughout the day to make sure that she is communicating adequately in other situations.

❑ Rehearse a question and answer before the group starts.

A child hogs the limelight

This is quite a tricky one. Confident she may seem but limelight hogging may be a sign of nervousness. Being on your knee during the session may help to keep her quiet while the others have a turn. Make sure she gets the opportunity to say her piece, though, and then encourage her to listen to the others' comments.

A child expresses anti-social opinions

Even if the comment itself is offensive, remember that it is highly likely to be a 'picked up' opinion. You are quite within your rights to express an opinion that contradicts the child's comment, but do so gently: 'Actually, Matthew, I don't agree with you that all women are stupid. I know some very clever people and many of them are women'.

❑ Make a note of the opinions the children express and evaluate your equal opportunities policies in the light of them.

Sample session

❑ Opening story – may have a moral or may be connected to your theme.

❑ Short discussion about the story and any issues it raises.

❑ Vocabulary time ('Who can tell me what 'x' might mean?' A word from the story would be ideal).

❑ Guided conversation and calm, quiet 'joining in' games. Choose items such as finger rhymes/ memory games/talking about stimulating pictures/making up stories together.

❑ Talk time – 'Has anyone got anything that they want to talk about?' Open discussion and conversation; you may like to include 'show and tell' here if you do not cover that during the registration session.

❑ Closing short story or poem.

❑ Quiet minute.

Assessment

Stepping stones towards the goal 'understand what is right and wrong and why'.

❑ Begins to accept the needs of others, with support.

❑ Shows care and concern for others, for living things and the environment.

❑ Shows confidence and the ability to stand up for own rights.

❑ Has an awareness of the boundaries set and behavioural expectations within the setting.

Choosing time

Choosing time, free play, play time - whatever you call these unstructured sessions, the idea is the same: the children choose an activity for themselves and play with it, ideally putting it away when they have finished. This is a time for learning how to play, how to choose, what you enjoy and how to cooperate with each other.

The High/Scope model

A method of teaching children to be responsible for their own choices and to carry through plans they have made was formed in the USA. It began as an experiment to research grass roots solutions for the increasing crime rates in certain areas. The programme was

Early Learning Goals

These activities will help you work towards the following goals:

❑ Be confident to try new activities, initiate ideas and speak in a familiar group.

❑ Form good relationships with adults and peers.

❑ Understand that they can expect others to treat their own needs, views, cultures and beliefs with respect.

❑ Work as part of a group or class, taking turns and sharing fairly, understanding that there needs to be agreed values and codes of behaviour for groups of people.

❑ Select and use activities and resources independently.

called Head Start. If children could be taught to feel responsible for their own actions, it was argued, they would be less likely to turn to crime as young adults. The experiment was a resounding success and from it came the High/Scope method of teaching young children.

The High/Scope model of early years education has developed a detailed schema for choosing time sessions. To operate a High/Scope nursery you need to have considerable further training but there are some basic principles which are easy to apply to most groups – especially in the management of choosing time.

The room is set up in advance with some activities on tables, the usual equipment such as sand and water trays, home corner, and so on, and the children have access to the store shelves for games, construction sets and puzzles.

In a small group, ideally with a key worker, the child looks at what is available for the day. The adult explains what is set out and what each activity involves. The child then chooses a number of activities (three is enough at once) and the adult puts a labelled sticker for each chosen activity on the child.

The child then goes off and independently organises herself to complete the tasks she has set herself. Staff in the room know where she is intending to be by the stickers on her jumper and will encourage her to complete what she set out to do.

If there is not enough room at one of her activities, she must go away and come back later, moving on to another of her choices.

Half-way through the session, the key worker group reforms and the children report back to their key worker. She asks if they have achieved their goals and, if not, she asks what the problem was. She suggests solutions and the child then goes back and tries to complete her chosen activities.

At the end of the session, the group reforms again and the children feed back their experiences, good and bad. They may tell the group how much they enjoyed one particular activity and why, or they may say that they didn't know how to join in a group already involved in something. The children support each other and suggest solutions for the next time. The adult helps the children round off the session with positive thoughts and plans for the next time.

The High/Scope teaching method relies on detailed and careful recording of the children's achievements, and the children's progress towards the target of independent planning is monitored closely. Although groups may not be trained to do this detailed record-keeping, it is possible to learn a great deal about the child's ability to make these complicated plans and follow through, an indication that the child is maturing emotionally and learning how to learn effectively by using existing observation methods during the structured choosing time.

Using the stickers and planning approach may not be appropriate for all groups for all sessions, but to have a 'sticker choosing time' two or three times a week will offer the children the chance to learn how to motivate and monitor themselves.

Choosing time themes

Having a choosing time theme that complements your main topic will help children to consolidate their learning. By setting out table-top activities and some floor games in advance, you can engineer the children's play to a certain degree, suggesting that they play specific games with each set of equipment. For example:

Seasons

❑ Creating seasonal pictures;

❑ Boating in the water tray;

❑ Building a beach scene in the sand;

❑ Building towers strong enough to withstand a winter storm;

❑ Setting up the play people to go on a summer holiday;

❑ Making a celebration party in the home corner.

Colour

Prompt children by saying:

❑ 'Choose toys and games with a blue/red/yellow sticker today'

or

❑ 'Take your toys from the blue/red/yellow box'.

Water

Children could:

❑ Build boats in the junk corner;

❑ Make houses on stilts out of Lego;

❑ Set up a marbling table;

❑ Cope with a flood in the home corner.

All about me

Children could:

❑ Find puzzles and games which have people as their theme;

❑ Set out the play people and dolls' houses;

❑ Make pipe-cleaner people or cut-out dolls;

❑ Build a giant in the junk corner;

❑ Build houses for your family from Lego or similar.

Planning for success

Choosing time should be planned for as any other activity would. Children should be encouraged to care for the equipment that they are playing with and to put it away.

Have a signal that requires children to stop what they are doing – useful if the noise level gets too high.

Warn children when the session is due to end so that they can finish what they are doing. Let the children finish what they are doing when you end the session, even if you have to leave someone in the corner busy with a building while the others go on to snack or outdoor play.

Assessment

Stepping stones towards the goal 'select and use activities and resources independently':

❑ Shows willingness to tackle problems and enjoy self chosen challenges.

❑ Demonstrates a sense of pride in own achievement

❑ Takes initiatives and manages developmentally appropriate tasks.

❑ Operates independently within the environment and shows confidence in linking up with others for support and guidance.

Allow children to keep models and things that they have made set up until the end of the session if they want to show the person who is collecting them.

Make sure you have enough adults to move around observing and helping if asked to without interfering with the children's own games.

Limit the number of children in popular areas and make sure that the children take turns fairly.

Personal, Social and Emotional Development

The home corner

There was a time when home corners were almost identical in every group. There were kitchens for girls to play in and car boxes for boys to play with. The girls played mummies in the home corner and the boys were allowed walk-on parts as daddy coming in from work. This has changed but you must not underestimate the effect that such play had on you when it was you in the home corner. If you are over 25, you will probably have to have relearned, intellectually and deliberately, skills and principles that you want the children in your care to grow up to accept as entirely natural.

What do you call it?

Home corner is now a misnomer in many ways. It is a slight improvement on Wendy house (where girls learned to play mother to lost boys and boys learned to be lost) but it is a limiting name for a wonderful area of play. Life skills area sounds cumbersome, theatre is relevant but confusingly already used. Naming such a wide-based resource is limiting it by nature. Play corner negates what is happening elsewhere in the group. How about marking the area with a boundary of some sort and calling it the red corner or the boxes area, the window corner or even the PSED area, which is in fact what it really is! PSED is a cryptic enough title not to limit the children to playing one situation. Whatever you decide, the decision process at a staff meeting will enable you all to be more aware of what the area is, in fact, for.

Learning about life

The PSED corner can be a source of great inspiration and good play experiences. It is one of the places where role play is most obvious and many children will dash to be the first in at the start of a session. It is perfect for examining life in different situations and acting out the different roles children see around them. Testing life in this way is at the heart of play and the single most valuable activity in which young children engage.

Lion cubs roll and cuff each other in play fights, learning how to defend themselves as adults. Kittens stalk a ball of wool, practising their hunting skills while children talk and act, cooperating with each other to become the complex social animal that is the human adult.

As an indicator of what is going on inside a child's mind, discreet observation during role play is invaluable. You know what you think is normal behaviour and if you are surprised by the behaviour that a particular child is exhibiting, take note and share your concern with a colleague. See if someone else agrees with you - remember that we all have a different understanding of 'normal'. If you both agree that the child's behaviour is worrying, you will need to plan for further investigation, according to the policy of your setting.

Early Learning Goals

These activities will help you work towards the following goals:

❑ Be confident to try new activities, initiate ideas and speak in a familiar group.

❑ Form good relationships with adults and peers.

❑ Understand that they can expect others to treat their own needs, views, cultures and beliefs with respect.

❑ Work as part of a group or class, taking turns and sharing fairly, understanding that there needs to be agreed values and codes of behaviour for groups of people, including adults and children to work together harmoniously.

❑ Select and use activities and resources independently.

❑ Dress and undress independently and manage their own hygiene.

❑ Have a developing awareness of their own needs, views, feelings and be sensitive to those of others.

❑ Have a developing respect for their own cultures and beliefs and those of others.

❑ Consider the consequences of words and actions for themselves and others.

Setting a scene

Setting a scene before the children arrive can be a good idea although sometimes it is nice to be able to predict what the game will be. Maybe you could have an occasional surprise day. You could set up specific incidents, give the children a background story and see what happens. If you were to ask the children to supply ideas for the next surprise, you would find that they are far less squeamish than you. Here are some suggestions that a group of four-year-olds came up with:

❑ Burglary – this house was burgled last night and they tipped everything out and took some of the special things...

❑ Royal visitor – this house is going to be visited by the queen today, we need to get ready...

❑ Infestation of beetles (use anything small and black to represent beetles – screwed-up tissue paper, for example) – escaped beetles have crawled into this house and are hiding everywhere. We need to get them out and collect them in a box to send back to the insect house at the zoo...

❑ Flooded house – put wet cardboard down on the floor, soak newspaper and leave it around, soak some cotton dressing-up clothes and have dryers ready when the children ask you for them. A tap leaked overnight and look what happened...

❑ Car crash – paint a large grocery carton as a car, tip it on its side and use soft toys or dolls as the victims. Oh no, look, a car crash, what shall we do...?

Let parents know what your plans are. They may well have valuable resources that they would be happy for you to use. They will also be able to tell you of any significant occurrences in a child's life which may affect your plans.

Exploring families

With the area set up as a house containing kitchen and dining equipment, babies in the form of dolls, small scale furniture and other props, the children can explore the day-to-day trivia of their lives and practise being grown-up. They can also site fears and phobias and explore some of the trauma of their lives in the relative security of your setting.

The new baby

By changing what is available to the home makers at play in the house, you can, to a certain extent, engineer what they will explore. Putting in new-born baby equipment will encourage

children to explore the arrival of a new child into a family. You will have to be prepared to allow them to play at giving birth, at displaying anger, jealousy and tiredness. Children will also want to play breast-feeding as well as nappy-changing - let them.

Celebrations

Make sure that you have dolls from different cultures. Have kitchen equipment that includes chop sticks and woks, pestles and mortars and open cooking pots on pretend fires. Organise festivals, weddings and celebrations from the home corner and encourage the children to plan for these special days. Ask them how they feel about the planning and preparation of these events (be honest, allow them to understand that planning for a happy event does not necessarily make you feel good!) and play the role of guest, giving them a real audience to play to.

Dressing-up clothes

The dressing-up clothes you have available will also change how the children play. You could have only one sort of clothes available on some days, smart outfits one day and ragged clothing the next. The children will incorporate this into their play and can be encouraged to take note of the different situations they choose to play. There are often two or three items of clothing that become favourites. You may need to help the children to share the clothes. There will always be some children who race to the rail, don the

item they want and wear it for the rest of that session. It is not unusual for some children to do this for months. There is no harm in a child enjoying one particular outfit but think carefully about what the reasons may be if it becomes obsessive. Repetitive obsessive behaviour is an indicator of possible problems.

Relationships

Family relationships are the source of much happiness and grief. In the home corner children will begin to explore how people who live together can negotiate, empathise and communicate. They will bring their own experiences with them and you will be able to see the children who come from a stable and loving home treating each other with respect and expressing their own needs clearly. Those who are more troubled will have greater difficulty. You need to be aware of the children who shy away from the home corner as much as you do those who obsessively play the same role day after day.

Your role

Your role is one of household goddess, or at least fairy godmother, in many ways. You can intervene and help children learn more about the best way to get on with their peers. You can change the story by effecting change in the environment but you should not be too involved or visible. If you have watched a problem evolve and you have seen the children trying and failing to sort it out, you could join in temporarily – 'OK children, let's pretend that it is the day before and that the bad thing hasn't happened yet. Let's change what happened and make today a better day.' Help them to get restarted and then retreat again. This emotional coaching will stand them in good stead.

Moving out of the home corner and involving the whole group in occasional, prepared-in-advance role-play events is great fun. Staged weddings, concerts, a birthday party for one of the toys or a make-believe person, even a visit by a 'local dignitary' (probably you in a hat!) offer learning opportunities of all kinds. Video tape the children playing one of these group games and enjoy it just as much the second (or 22nd!) time around. If you have a video player, you can play at TV programmes – tapes of the children telling jokes or doing a weather forecast is easy to set up, or you could simply video them playing. Seeing yourself on TV is a great education and helps support personal development in its search for a basic self-knowledge – what you look like is a good place to start.

If your home corner is too precious to you and the children and you would miss it by trying out the other scenarios appropriate for exploration, or if you have children in your group who, for one reason or another, consistently need to play out important issues in a house-based role-play corner – then have two! Better still, have two or three linked areas – a factory, a shop and a house; an emergency vehicle rescuing accident victims and a hospital; a card factory and a birthday party role-play. You will come back to the home corner again and again and rightly so, this is the time that children learn most from their home environment. However, ignoring the other possibilities completely is a mistake.

Exploring health issues

Illness, death, pain and fear are frightening for all of us, not just children. There will be children in your group who have experienced these issues, to a lesser or greater extent, and they will all remember them. Playing out these fears and experiences will help the children to come to terms with the harsher facts of life and give you the opportunity to slay some dragons in the process. Fear of the unknown can create some terrible potential scenarios in the minds of children who, for example, are going to hospital for a simple routine operation and you will be able to reassure the child about what is going to happen. Using the vets as a less contentious issue may seem to be easier. Always let parents know your plans beforehand so that they have time to let you know of any life dramas that particular children have

experienced recently and you should know about.

Hospital

Bandages, slings, beds, blankets, torch for looking down throats and in ears, stethoscopes, thermometers, plastic syringes, charts to write on and hospital staff uniforms (unisex please!).

Vets

Soft toys as patients, boxes for the animals to be brought in, food and water bowls, a table for the vet to examine and treat the animal on, plastic syringes, eye and ear drops (dropper bottles are available from large chemists), leads, a waiting area.

Exploring the essentials and the extras in life

Visiting the shops, choosing what to spend money on, interacting with the strangers in the various places that grown-ups visit and watching what goes on in these places will encourage a child to take note of the world around

him. There is maths and science, language and literacy, manual dexterity, creative skills, new knowledge and an understanding of the real world in every one of these role-play activities. Personal, social and emotional development is the glue that holds this together.

Shop

Empty packets, cartons and tins (not opened), weighing scales, loose products (potatoes are easy) to be weighed, paper bags, hardware such as dusters and mops, newspapers and magazines, carrier bags to take the shopping away in, a till and money. Using real coppers and low value coins is perfect.

Post office/bank

Paper, envelopes, stickers for stamps, a variety of stamps and ink pads, information leaflets, weighing scales, parcels to be wrapped, wrapping paper, string and sticky tape to wrap them, money, books with tear-out pages (scrap paper cut into rectangles and

stapled at one end), a post box, telephones, counter and money drawer.

Pet shop

Soft toy animals for sale, boxes as cages, empty cartons of food, toys for pets, leads and collars (string or lengths of ribbon will do), bowls, dog bones (twist newspaper into a bone shape), food bowls and water bowls, shredded paper as bedding, a till.

Café

Tables and chairs, tablecloths, napkins, crockery and cutlery, a trolley, notepad for taking orders, pretend food (or healthy snacks), teapots, menus, flowers on the table, a till.

Fish and chip shop

Counter, fish (papier mache fish are easy to make, roll them in glue and sawdust for breadcrumbs), chips (cardboard is fine, wooden ones are easy to make and much better), paper squares for wrapping (newspaper is fine, although it is not allowed in shops

any more!), empty vinegar and ketchup bottles, salt shakers, price list, till and money.

Hairdresser's

Rollers, combs and brushes, empty spray containers or water-filled ones, mirrors, chairs, clips, slides and hair elastics, a hairdryer.

Shoe shop

Pairs of shoes of all sizes, boxes, measuring slides (rectangles of wood with marks on and a section of dressmaker's measuring tape to measure width) or recreate your own electronic version from recycled materials, carrier bags, till and money.

Creativity in everyday life

Creativity as an isolated activity is a great loss in everyday life. Making something is therapeutic. Cooperating with others and putting your work on display is one aspect of creativity that this activity will explore. Pride in the result is important but so is the knowledge that it is your own work – don't cheat children of this, let them do it.

Gift shop

Set up a 'behind the scenes' table where children can make quick gifts and a shop to sell them in. If you choose a craft gift that needs to dry, plan ahead and do them the day before. Ideas include:

❑ Tissue paper flowers

❑ Decorated flower pots

❑ Decorated badges

❑ Lavender bags

❑ Bead jewellery

❑ Wooden flowers (pre-cut shapes to glue together)

❑ Ornaments from painted stones and tied twigs

❑ Greetings cards

❑ Perfume (Have several small bottles with water in. Add a few drops of food colouring and some safe scent such as lavender or lemon.)

Discuss what the customer would like and why and then wrap it prettily.

The world of work

Work is a contentious issue - some families have none, some have too much. Work can mean being separated from your parents for quite long stretches of time and it is also where many of the children in your care are heading for as adults. This is an important area to explore. Tell parents what you are doing and ask them to let the children know what they do in the day.

Office

Phones, paper, pens, calculators, rulers, filing boxes, stickers, stamps and ink pads, leaflets, scissors, paper-clips, sticky tape, desks and chairs.

Garage

Use the trikes and scooters as your customers' vehicles and fix them with plastic tools. Using real tools on wheeled toys is not a good idea but if you have any old wheeled toys you no longer use then real tools are wonderful.

Repair shop

Have broken things, such as clocks, boxes, pots and pans, old radios (without the batteries), crockery, and so on, and then offer tools for fixing things.

Factory

A production line making something like a pompon or assembling a pre-designed Lego car helps you to explore cooperation. If your community is reliant on one particular manufacturing employer, see if you can recreate the world of work that the children will be used to hearing about.

Exploring further afield

This is still a strange idea to young

children for whom the world has only just extended to include nursery or pre-school! Just after the long holidays, though, when memories are still relatively fresh, these ideas may help the children to explore and express recent experience.

Airport check-in

Tickets (rectangles of paper taped together and the name of the destination in large bold marker on the front), baggage, labels, boarding cards, pens, paper and a blackboard sign that makes the destination clear.

Travel agents

Brochures from holiday companies, pens, paper, phones, tickets, chairs and desks. The customers can look through brochures, choose a picture that appeals and arrange to go there.

Somewhere to hide

There is something exciting about being able to hide in a crowded place. Let children build a den from old sheets and a clothes dryer and furnish it with items from the junk box.

Somewhere to explore the imagination

Scene-building is an important factor here. You may like to read stories that reflect the scene you have built - this

will help to kick start the game. Make sure that you build with health and safety in mind.

Moonscape

Put bubble wrap on the floor, drape blue fabric around the area studded with tinfoil stars to recreate a lunar landscape. A confined area to represent a space shuttle will enhance the life of this scene considerably. Have pretend buttons to press, radios, boxes covered in tinfoil as machines, supply boxes with face pieces cut out and all-in-one suits to wear.

Fairy glade

Ideally, this should take place outside. Alternatively, try putting a rug down and drape green material around the walls. Toadstools out of little stools are perfect (large garden pots turned upside down will do). Put flowers in pots in the area and provide wispy net and gauze for dressing up in. Have a grown-up fairy cloak ready to be fairy queen, the storyteller…

Under the sea

Blue net, large stones and green strips of tissue as seaweed hanging from above create the base for this wonderful scenario. Driftwood, cardboard starfish, tinfoil tropical fish and baskets of sea shells finish the effect.

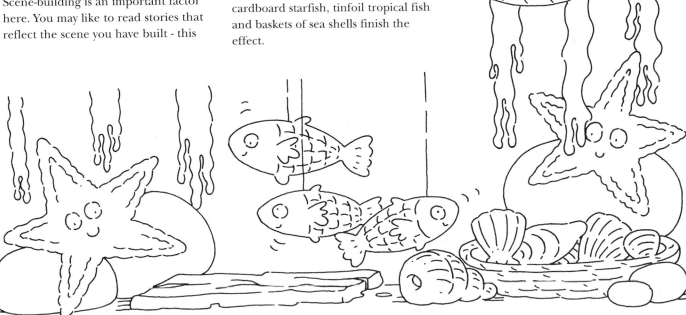

Personal, Social
and **Emotional Development**

Learning to share

There are some things that children should not have to share. They should not have to share things that are precious to them, such as a comforter or an item that they do not believe will be cared for by the person they are supposed to be sharing it with. They have to be able to trust that the person they are sharing one of their own possessions with will respect it and return it in one piece. There are several things that adults would not consider sharing and we must allow children the same rights.

Children need to learn how to interact with others and one of the ways that social interaction begins is by sharing. We share a smile, a greeting, an introduction, an initial conversation, then perhaps a cup of coffee and, as we share our experiences and time with another, we find ourselves with friends. Sharing is one of the ways we link ourselves to others.

Sharing out communal items (such as playdough, biscuits, sweets) fairly so that all can have an equal share and still enjoy it is easy. Sharing out communal items that can only be used by one person at a time such as a popular toy, is less easy and requires patience and trust on the part of the child who has to wait for their turn.

The children in the group who were the first child in the family may well be facing the hardest lesson of all - sharing parents with a new baby. They will be feeling under pressure and unsettled because they are not the only one. Not sharing well at nursery is a common response to this insecurity.

Early Learning Goals

❑ Form good relationships with adults and peers.

❑ Understand that they can expect others to treat their own needs, views, cultures and beliefs with respect.

❑ Work as part of a group or class, taking turns and sharing fairly, understanding that there needs to be agreed values and codes of behaviour for groups of people, including adults and children to work together harmoniously.

❑ Have a developing respect for their own cultures and beliefs and those of other people.

❑ Understand that people have different needs, views, cultures and beliefs, which need to be treated with respect.

❑ Understand what is right and wrong and why.

❑ Consider the consequences of words and actions for themselves and others.

Sharing out something like a cake is a great maths learning opportunity. Dividing up a collection of items such as grapes, raisins or sweets and counting out who has how many is an excellent counting experience. Sharing your new toy car is a Personal, Social and Emotional Development milestone that takes the same sort of support and preparation.

Make sure that you notice and reward the child who shares a toy, but also make sure that a child can say no, politely, to a request from another child that she is not happy to comply with.

You can practise sharing in many different ways.

The mystery box

'Just today, as I was on my way to play with you, I found a box. I don't know what is in the box but here it is, all wrapped up in beautiful paper. I would like to share this box with you but I can't think of a way for six of us to share one box! Can you?'

Suggestions:

❑ Take it in turns to guess what is in it.

❑ Choose someone to open it.

❑ Let the children pick a paper each out of the hat; the child who picks the one with a cross on it unwraps the box.

❑ One person unwraps it and another opens it.

What is a fair way for us all to share this? Is it as much fun watching as it is actually unwrapping it?

By this time, the children will have come up with some solutions. Choose one of them, make sure you have a unanimous decision and follow through.

You need to have put in the box beforehand something easy to share out that all the children can enjoy as a reward for sharing so well!

Pass the parcel

This is the perfect game for taking turns. Make something of each layer of paper as it comes off by adding a forfeit such as a rhyme, turn around, clap five times, and so on, and ensure that everyone has a go at getting a forfeit.

You can have a group activity in the parcel instead of a traditional present. It could be a clue as to what is going to happen next:

❑ A wellington boot – playing outside;

❑ A paintbrush – paint time;

❑ A cup – snack time;

❑ A new book – story time.

The Little Red Hen

Stories with a moral, such as 'The Little Red Hen', are useful as an introduction to the idea of sharing workloads as well as possessions. In other words, helping.

Read the story and talk about what has happened, how the hen feels, how the pig and the duck and the dog feel and whether it is fair or not. Children have a well developed sense of justice (if rather unilateral at times!) and will usually have an opinion on this.

Then act out the story with simple props. The hen should ask nicely for help and the farmyard friends should turn her down. She carries on and makes the bread and then will not share it. Should she have shared it?

Replay the tale again and this time let the hen share the bread, even though her friends did not deserve it. Is this better? How did the hen feel? Did she enjoy the bread any more when she had it all for herself? Did she still have enough bread, even though she shared

it? Maybe the other animals learn a lesson from her kindness?

Avoid preaching here if you can. Try to get the children to explore the possibilities on their own. Don't react to the child who refuses to accept any compromise and cannot countenance the possibility that the hen might share anyway. The idea is that you are encouraging the children to realise that they have choices in life and the way to a fulfilled life is not always the obvious one.

Team games

Competition is avoided in many schools where losing is considered too great a blow to confidence to inflict on children. Others choose to make the acts of winning and losing lessons in life skills. Consistent losing is awful, consistent winning does no-one any good in the long run and team work is how most of us end up spending our days whether we are working at home or out of it. The idea that people must cooperate and all pull together towards one goal is a good one. Party games are all about finding winners and schools that still have sports days find them to be a popular event. As with all of the lessons that children learn at school, some will need more support and help to achieve than others, but winning or beating a personal best

record makes anyone justifiably proud.

Team games for young children must be simple and require cooperation. Just a little bit of results rigging won't hurt either so that the children all get a turn at losing and winning. This is the ultimate in sharing!

❑ Obstacle courses;

❑ Races;

❑ Hunt the thimble (or any other smallish item) in teams;

❑ Charades;

❑ Quizzes.

With enough adults to hand, you can ensure that every child is praised for either beating a personal record, getting something right that they got wrong before, being in the winning team, being nearest to the hidden thimble most frequently (even if they never found it!) and you can engineer these events into positive experiences for all concerned.

Assessment

Stepping stones towards the goal 'consider the consequences of their words and actions for themselves and others'.

❑ Begins to accept the needs of others, with support

❑ Shows care and concern for others, for living things and the environment.

❑ Shows confidence and the ability to stand up for own rights.

❑ Has an awareness of the boundaries set and behavioural expectations within the setting.

Personal, Social
and **Emotional Development**

Wait for it!

A psychological test of emotional maturity was reported in the national press. The marshmallow test, an indicator of a child's ability to hold back and control initial desires, can apparently be used to suggest emotional intelligence.

In the test the adult puts a marshmallow on a table in front of a four-year-old. The child is given the choice to either have the sweet immediately or to wait 20 minutes, in which case he or she will be allowed to have two.

The test was carried out on groups of children over several years and the children were measured for various social and emotional skills at different stages. The children who were able to resist the initial offer of the single sweet at four years old were more likely to be emotionally more stable and mature later on in their childhood than the ones who could not wait.

Waiting patiently comes more easily to some of us than others. Supermarket queues, touch-tone phone queues and traffic jams are all part of everyday life and we can all feel our blood pressure rising at some stage. Being able to wait patiently and calmly for something that you want requires several issues to be sorted first:

❑ Trust that you will get the desired outcome in the end;

❑ Understanding that waiting will not detract from the end result;

❑ An ability to understand that waiting

Early Learning Goals

❑ Form good relationships with adults and peers.

❑ Work as part of a group or class, taking turns and sharing fairly, understanding that there needs to be agreed values and codes of behaviour for groups of people, including adults and children, to work together harmoniously.

❑ Have a developing awareness of their own needs, views and feelings and be sensitive to those of others.

❑ Consider the consequences of words and actions for themselves and others.

❑ Maintain attention, concentrate and sit quietly when appropriate.

---

is part of everyday life;

❑ An ability not to feel victimised by the wait itself.

Learning to wait patiently without becoming angry or anxious is important for future happiness and good health. Begin with making waiting an activity in itself.

The waiting game

Just for fun, wait for something. A story, for example. When the children are settled and ready, suggest that you all wait for the story: 'Let's wait for ten seconds, shall we?' Then count up to ten slowly before beginning the story.

'Our snacks are not quite ready. Just for fun, shall we wait patiently and listen to the noises outside?'

'In one minute it will be outside play time. Let's wait here and sing a song, shall we?'

'What a queue for the bathroom! Does anyone know a joke/rhyme/song to tell us while we wait?'

At the train station

There are many good activities which involve you playing with trains. You could have a cardboard box with a hole in the base for the engine and others for the carriages for the children to make the train. You might then form a conga line behind this train and all join on as the line stops at a station. The children might be in groups around the room, waiting for their name to be called so that they can jump aboard. You could have a long rope, knotted at regular intervals to mark where each new passenger holds on (you will need an adult at the back to stop you all tripping over the rope trailing behind you). These are good cooperative games and children will be waiting, listening for their name. If they are not waiting patiently, their name might not be called out. As the driver (you) pulls up at a station, look at the waiting children and see if they are waiting well. If they are, they can jump aboard.

Listening skills, understanding instructions, waiting for turns and moving in cooperation with others are all covered in this fun activity.

Countdown

Choose something each week that you will decide to wait for.

❑ Post a letter to the group with a new story or an interesting picture in it. Tell the children early in the week that you are expecting it and are going to wait for it. Don't post it until midweek so that when it arrives the children will have been waiting two or three days.

❑ Choose one of the activities planned for the end of the week and describe it in detail to the group. Then explain how long the wait will be.

❑ Plan a different snack for one of the days and wait for that day to come.

If you do this, make sure that the promised treat happens, ignore any impatience in the waiting time and remind the children every day that they are waiting.

Calendars

Calendars are complicated ideas to young children. They require a number recognition that matches a knowledge of the days of the week and an ability to understand further ahead than tomorrow or further behind than yesterday.

Start with tomorrow and yesterday. Have a three-day calendar on a board that will accommodate three good-sized pieces of paper alongside each other. This activity will take a few days to complete. Remove the oldest page when you get to day three and begin each week with a clean calendar board.

Day one – write the name of the day on the top of the paper and stick a picture on that day to represent an activity that the children have all done on that day.

Day two – look at the paper and remember yesterday. Add another piece of paper to the board with a picture on for today. Discuss an activity that you have planned for the next day and write a simple single word on the paper for tomorrow to remind you what you are planning.

Day three – what did you have planned for today? What did you do yesterday? What did you do the day before yesterday? Would anyone like to suggest the story for tomorrow and we can write it on the paper for tomorrow?

Extension idea

Use a page-a-week diary and let the children draw in a record of what they did each day. Plan ahead for a week or so and ask the children to see how many days it is until a specific treat.

Birthdays and festivals

Planning for a birthday or Christmas Day reduces many small children to nervous, tearful creatures. A calm acceptance that something good is going to happen without the stress and excitement resulting in tears and tantrums is learned by example as much as anything else. Christmas is a wonderful time for many children. Going too far and exhausting everyone will remove the magic that children feel quite naturally at the beginning of this festive season. Nurture the wonder but do not exhaust the child.

Birthday candles

Why not have mini Advent calendars for the week before a birthday? A five-day countdown will help the child put each day of waiting in place and the idea that you are moving slowly towards the big day helps the child stay calm. You may well have several different birthday calendars on the go at any time, so keep them quite small.

In a rectangular piece of wood (30 cm x 10 cm x 2 cm) drill five shallow holes along the middle. Fit five dowels in, no longer than a pencil. Make several candles out of cardboard tubes and decorate them with stickers and shiny material. Make the bright flame out of yellow or orange cardboard. Have a box of candles for the children to choose from.

Carve a long slit along the front of the candle holder in which to put the child's name on a piece of cardboard.

Each day of the five days before the big day, the child can add a candle to the holder. Number work becomes much more attractive this way and waiting becomes part of the celebration.

You can buy candle holders if you prefer. Set up one for each year of the child's age and let the child put an unlit candle in each holder, one a day. On the day, light the candles and the child can blow them out.

Assessment

Stepping stones towards the goal 'maintain attention, concentrate and sit quietly when appropriate'.

❑ Shows curiosity.

❑ Has a strong exploratory impulse.

❑ Has a positive approach to new experiences.

❑ Shows increasing independence in selecting and carrying out activities.

❑ Shows confidence in linking up with others for support and guidance.

❑ Displays high levels of involvement in activities.

❑ Persists for extended periods of time at an activity of their choosing.

❑ Takes risks and explores within the environment.

Facing up to fears

The world can be a frightening place for young children. One of the main targets of early years education is to help children begin to make sense of the world around them, and reduce some of that fear.

Children, like adults, are predominantly afraid of what they don't understand. They are afraid of things they can't explain, things they

Early Learning Goals

❑ Be confident to try new activities, initiate ideas and speak in a familiar group.

❑ Continue to be interested, excited and motivated to learn.

❑ Select and use activities and resources independently.

❑ Have a developing respect for their own needs, views and feelings and be sensitive to those of others.

❑ Respond to significant experiences showing a range of feelings when appropriate.

can't see and they easily absorb the fears of the adults around them. They are afraid of being hurt, abandoned, lonely and, most of all, they are afraid of being afraid.

Facing fear is a sweet and sour experience. There is a frisson about knowing that you are going to do something that might make you scared and yet the high felt by a child who has faced a fear and won is unmatched.

Abstract fears such as the fear of abandonment is cured by a growing surety that the child's world is, in fact, safe and that she will not be abandoned because she is loved and valued. Fairy stories which are quite gruesome, such as *Hansel and Gretel*, help the child to face this fear.

Fear of speaking out or of rejection are cured by the careful nurturing at home and at school of each child's new sense of self-esteem and self-value and, over time, recurrent positive experiences.

More specific fears can be addressed as individual activities in a safe and supportive atmosphere. Don't expect miracles, but do understand that every little step towards coping with a fear, even if it seems overwhelming, is a step on the road to self-confidence and independence.

Dark dens

Being afraid of the dark is common. Many children will not go to sleep without the light on and many more

will scream if they wake up in the dark. Some families start young and always put their baby to bed in the dark, feeding and comforting him in the dark to reassure that there is nothing to be afraid of. Other children can be three or four and never have been in the dark at all. This is quite understandable – as is the probable fear of the dark that is likely to accompany such an experience.

Find a fairly dark corner or build a den and take a torch in. The children who are not afraid will find this great fun and those who are may be tempted to do something that they wouldn't do otherwise because of the infectious nature of another's enjoyment. Practise turning the torch on and off, talk about how the den is the same if there is light or not and slowly encourage the afraid child to play in the darkened place.

Read the story *Can't You Sleep, Little Bear?* by Martin Waddell and Barbara Firth (Walker). Little Bear is frightened of the dark. When it comes

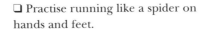

to bedtime he can't get to sleep. Big Bear finds an ingenious way to reassure him.

Spiders

Psychologists argue that we may be pre-programmed to be afraid of animals that could harm us, such as spiders and snakes, and a healthy respect for insects that sting or bite is a valuable tool.

Although spiders in this country are safe, the fear of them is quite paralysing to lots of people and facing a live spider may well be too tall an order. There are, of course, as many children who love spiders and would collect and handle even the large black hairy ones that have some grown-ups running for cover!

❑ Make spiders out of black wool pompons and pipe-cleaner legs.

❑ Paint, print (sponge circles and legs) and draw spiders.

❑ Practise running like a spider on hands and feet.

❑ Sing songs about spiders ('Incy Wincy' being the favourite) and make your fingers climb like a spider.

❑ Face paint a spider's face on the back of your hand and make your fingers crawl like a spider.

Wasps and bees

These insects come under the 'maintain a healthy respect for' variety! Being calm when one is near, not staying covered in sticky ice lolly in July and not flapping at them when they are close is common sense. An adult's fear is in many ways more frightening than the object of fear itself so, even if you are afraid, play it cool!

Make wasps from cardboard rolls painted with stripes and add straw or pipe-cleaner legs and feelers and paper wings (a rectangle of paper, smaller than the roll and partially stuck onto the top of the wasp is easy and effective and manageable by the children).

Thunder and lightning

There is more nonsense talked in the explanation of thunder and lightning than almost anything else! God falling over, angels marching, giants' footsteps - it is no wonder that children are afraid! A simple but real explanation is always best. Thunder is the noise that the lightning makes as it crackles. It is delayed because noise travels more slowly than light - at one mile per second - so you see the flash first before you hear it. This is why you can tell how far away a storm is by counting between the flash and the noise. Lightning is caused by changes in the weather.

Monsters

Monsters allow us to give our worst fears terrible faces and worse bodies. How much easier it is to hate a monster than what is really worrying us!

Have fun with monsters as inspiration for art. The very act of making something as frightening as possible can be therapeutic.

Assessment

Stepping stones towards the goal 'continue to be interested, excited and motivated to learn'

❑ Shows curiosity.

❑ Has a strong exploratory impulse.

❑ Has a positive approach to new experiences.

❑ Shows increasing independence in selecting and carrying out activities.

❑ Shows confidence in linking up with others for support and guidance.

❑ Displays high levels of involvement in activities.

❑ Persists for extended periods of time at an activity of their choosing

❑ Takes risks and explores within the environment.

Personal, Social and Emotional Development

Mirror faces

Body language is an important aspect of communication. Skilled communicators and conversationalists read more signs than others and use them as a key to the real message behind the spoken words. Facial expressions are, perhaps, the first signs we learn to read. Expressionless people are hard to communicate with as an important aspect of the feedback required to make social interaction work is missing. People who are close to each other can read the slightest change in expression clearly and many mothers will know by one glance at a child's face how they are feeling.

Reading these signs is learned early. Children mimic facial expressions from about six months old. Beginning by smiling and laughing, then shaking or nodding the head, then frowns and more complex faces, the child learns

---

Early Learning Goals

❑ Consider the consequences of words and actions for themselves and others.

❑ Respond to significant experiences showing a range of feelings when appropriate.

❑ Maintain attention, concentrate and sit quietly when appropriate.

---

what these emotions mean. A smile at a baby is soon rewarded with one back while a frown and a shake of the head is enough to make many babies cry. No response or a blank face in response to a baby's smile will confuse and agitate the child. A child brought up in a group or large family will learn early about expressing needs and desires and may well, if supported and

encouraged, go on to be emotionally more literate than an isolated child or one who was too often ignored.

Emotional coaching

When children get cross with each other in your group, don't instantly react by telling them to stop it. If the situation has deteriorated into physical violence, you will want to separate the children but then diffuse the situation by saying calmly 'I see that you are both angry. Can you tell me why?'. Gently unravel what happened and turn a fisticuffs into an 'emotional coaching' session.

If children are laughing, get them to tell you what has amused them and enjoy it, too. If they are upset or look angry, encourage them to tell you what the problem is. If you create an atmosphere of expressing feelings safely, you will find that physical violence and its counterpart, withdrawn silence, both difficult to handle, are far less prevalent. You must allow children to be angry and teach them how to express it safely without punching or hitting. One of the key features in good emotional coaching is predictability and reliability on the part of parents and carers – make sure you are a secure base from which children will learn to spring.

The mirror game

Give each child a plastic mirror (or one between two). With the children in pairs, tell a short story as an introduction to a particular emotion and then pull the face that expresses that feeling. Discuss this as you go and

make sure that the children agree with your interpretation of how one might feel in that situation.

Retell the story more than once and encourage the children to mimic the emotion to each other and in the mirror.

Have some of the children be your faces for the story: as you read, their face will reflect the emotions expressed in the story. This game will work with many of the popular stories available today.

For the readers in your group, some simple cards that say 'happy', 'sad', 'angry', 'afraid', 'hurt', and so on, will add an extra dimension to this activity. Hold one up and, without speaking, they make the face that corresponds to the card.

Look through newspapers and magazines for photos of people expressing emotion and build up a resource file of these faces for discussion. With older children, you can even make up stories as to why they are feeling the way they are.

Emotions in popular stories

Here is a small sample of the hundreds of books that would be useful for this activity:

❑ *Where the Wild Things Are* by Maurice Sendak (Harper Trophy) ISBN 0-06-443178-9

Being told off (anger, shame), escape (relief), new places (excitement), monsters (fear), praise and adoration (pride),

homesickness (sadness), returning home (calmness, happiness).

❑ *What's that Noise?* Simon & Melling (Hodder) ISBN 0-340-65673-5

Strange places (excitement, fear, insecurity), strange noises (fear), explanations (relief), reassurance (happiness).

❑ *Five Minutes Peace* Jill Murphy (Walker) ISBN 0-7445-0491-0

How does mum feel? (empathy), children left out (rejection, sadness), being called a baby (cross), relaxation (peaceful, happy), being interrupted (cross), giving a gift (pleasure), boisterous time (fun for some).

❑ *Owl Babies* Martin Waddell (Walker) ISBN 0-7445-3167-5

Being at home (security), being left (fear, worry, sadness), waiting (anticipation, worry), reassuring each other (reassuring yourself, empathy), in the dark (fear), mother returns (relief, joy).

❑ *Lollopy* Dunbar Varley (Carnival) ISBN 0-261-67165-0

Being somewhere unsafe (fear, excitement), losing Lollopy (grief, guilt), Lollopy alone (fear, discomfort, sadness), the bogey rabbit (fear), being found (relief, joy), joining in (camaraderie, happiness), being left again (abandonment), young rabbits (guilt, fear, shame), next morning (being sorry, being brave).

Assessment

Stepping stones for the goal 'respond to significant experiences showing a range of feelings when appropriate'.

❑ Separates from main carer with support.

❑ Separates from main carer with confidence.

❑ Has a sense of belonging.

❑ Shows care and concern for self.

❑ Talks freely about their home and community.

❑ Has a sense of self as a member of different communities.

❑ Expresses needs and feelings in appropriate ways.

❑ Initiates interactions with other people.

Travelling Tara

Tara is a doll. This particular Tara is a readily available rag doll but she could be any doll, provided she is sturdy and appealing. She is a traveller and enjoys nothing more than going to different places and having adventures there.

She goes home with a different child once or twice a week and finds out about how different families live. She could go on holiday with them, to hospital, to parties or anywhere her host is going. As most serious travellers tend to do, Tara keeps a diary. Someone who can write, the host, or the host's parent or bigger brother or sister writes a few lines about what Tara has done on her visit and when she comes back to nursery, she can tell everyone about it.

Tara's diary is now an impressive document. She has photos of herself at parties, in hospital, playing with other children and in bed in various houses. She has a passport (stamped by immigration and signed by the pilot, of course) and photos of herself on holiday. She makes new friends wherever she goes and is a popular house guest with children queuing up to take her home. Several of her hosts have added to her wardrobe and the contents of her small red suitcase are now a testament to the dedication of several mums and dads.

Tara is lucky because the children who attend her nursery are well supported and encouraged to benefit from experiences such as the Tara project.

Although some groups may require more staff support than others, there are few settings which would not enjoy the insights and opportunities that a similar project would offer.

Children who have been hospitalised come back and explain to the group that Tara was a bit frightened, had to have an injection and found the bed uncomfortable. Children who have had parties and treats have stopped to consider Tara and included her as a guest. She has been shared with siblings and friends and her suitcase of clothes and equipment has been cared for and returned. Children have looked at their home lives through her eyes and shared some of the information with friends and staff at nursery. Talking about what Tara has

done and what Tara thinks is, as any child counsellor will testify, much easier than baring your own soul.

New horizons

Tara has brought new opportunities to the language and literacy curriculum as the children see the value of the written word as a communication tool and find their own words to describe to the group how Tara got on at their home.

Widening the group's knowledge and understanding of the world is an easy target with such a traveller in their midst and the personal and social opportunities that the Tara project has opened up have been excellent as children wait for their turn and make the most of her visit in order to have something to share.

Tara's needs have encouraged young children to empathise, a difficult skill to introduce. The very fact that Tara exists to travel has sown new ideas in the minds of many children and an awareness of the life she leads and the opportunities she has is an education in itself, an important understanding of a different way of life.

The original Tara project quickly became an important part of the nursery day and its usefulness continues. To keep the interest of more than one group of children, larger nurseries may need to launch more than one traveller. Roving Roger is now on Tara's circuit and they have been known to meet at birthday parties and other social events! Together they support the learning of more children, in more situations than many other projects could have done.

The resources required are minimal. Tara herself needs very little except a note book for a diary. The original Tara now has a suitcase, mobile phone, sun cream, passport, shoes, slippers (summer and winter) and an enviable array of clothes, some of them bought and made for her by her hosts. Each project will develop its own personality and soon reflect the culture that the children are living in. The insight that Tara brings staff and other children alike is invaluable. Getting to know the families of your children is not always easy and this is an ideal way to break the ice, without putting pressure on anyone.

A parent-led project that requires the minimum of organisation from you is an efficient and valuable addition to any setting that actively encourages parental involvement. As always, sympathetic handling may be required to support parents who for some reason are not able to contribute and some imaginative support might be required for some families, but this is an inclusive project that is well within the reach of the vast majority of people.

Staff may well decide to take Tara home now and again. You might like to put in a photo of Tara on your kitchen table or in your garden. Children love to hear about the home lives of their teachers and are encouraged to find details in their own experience that others might be interested in. Tara might join a child at their first visit to 'big school' and report back to the group. Maybe your local shop or postal worker would take Tara for a few hours? The opportunities are endless!

Links with Personal, Social and Emotional Development

❑ Confidence in new activities, initiating ideas and speaking to a familiar group – reporting back on Tara's time at home and bringing new information back to the group.

❑ Forming good relationships with adults and peers – empathising with others, via Tara, and listening to others' experiences.

❑ Understanding that they can expect others to treat their own needs, views, cultures and beliefs with respect – feeling sure that the information about home life that Tara brings to the group will be treated with respect.

❑ Working as part of a group or class, taking turns and sharing fairly – waiting for it to be your turn to take Tara home.

❑ Understanding that there needs to be agreed values and codes of behaviour for groups of people to work together harmoniously – taking care of shared and valuable resources, like Tara's equipment.

❑ Being interested and excited – sharing these feelings with others when a long awaited turn comes around.

❑ Considering the consequences of words and actions for themselves and others – understanding that failing to return Tara or to lose or damage her equipment will directly affect others in the group.

❑ Responding to significant experiences, showing a range of feelings when appropriate – sharing news of good and bad times in the lives of others and thinking about how they feel can be the first step.

With thanks to Buttercups Kindergarten, Calne, Wiltshire, for this idea.

Dressing games

Being able to care for yourself starts with communicating your needs; it moves on to feeding and toileting and then comes the complicated stuff – buttons and zips! This progression is important - don't run before you can walk.

Start simply and play with hats and scarves. Babies often love hats and by pre-school age children are usually quite adept. Scarves make wonderful capes, dresses, cloaks or even wings but watch that they aren't pulled too tightly. Offering children real clothes to practise with is an obvious first step to dressing oneself. Their own clothes are already on, practice clothes can be bigger and just go over the top, removing some of the angst of being responsible for one's own clothes.

Practice clothes should be slightly too large, recognisable as ordinary clothes and have a variety of fastenings. Keep them in the dressing-up box to use alongside the more exotic costumes on offer.

Life skills, independence and pride in success are crucial boosters to self-esteem. Being able to manage tasks alone opens up a new world. Starting school able to manage your own clothes immediately gives the child confidence and a feeling that they can cope, that they are in control.

The most important thing you can give a child trying out these new and complicated fine motor skills is time. Take the pressure off, let them sit quietly and keep trying to do up a

Early Learning Goals

❑ Continue to be interested, excited and motivated to learn.

❑ Dress and undress independently and manage their own hygiene.

❑ Maintain attention, concentrate and sit quietly when appropriate.

button. They will be absorbed and totally committed to the task and the big sigh and flushed cheeks of eventual success are worth waiting for. Step in if the job is becoming too frustrating but reassure the child that she did well and tried hard – 'I bet you'll be doing this all on your own soon!'

If your group goes swimming or gets changed for PE sessions, allow a lot of extra time for getting dressed. Think about enlisting extra help or parents as volunteers for these occasions.

Expect the children to put on their own paint smocks and make sure that the design of the smock makes it easy to get on and off.

Involve parents, ask them how much help the child needs in the morning and evening and work together on small, achievable targets, especially if the child is reaching school age and still in need of assistance. Have a look at what the problem is, see if you can recreate it in a non-stressful scenario (using special cushions and dolls) and practise the skill. It may well be a small motor skill problem. Make sure that you are offering enough practice with construction blocks, dough, threading, cutting, and so on.

Specific items of equipment are available for practising fastenings on. Button and zip cushions and dolls with life-size fastenings on their clothes are useful resources although many children will not need them. The real clothes practice and time to succeed on their own is usually enough.

If you feel that star charts are useful incentives for being able to do specific tasks and if you feel that they encourage the children to try harder, then use them. You might consider keeping them a private matter and allowing the

child to show off his chart to the person who collects him if they want to.

Laces and coats

Tying shoelaces is one of those skills that suddenly you can just do. There are rhymes and sayings to help a child remember what to do – 'Chase the bunny around the tree and pop him in his hole' – but it really is a matter of patience and practice. Laces on boards and cut-out cardboard shoe shapes may help some children but there is nothing better than succeeding on the real thing so use shoes as much as possible.

The advent of Velcro means that children can avoid tying laces for years. However, tying laces is still a skill that needs to be learned at some point, so have a go, see how you get on and if the child just can't do it, wait a while and try again.

Coats are a different matter. Children nearly always need coats and they need to be done up. Putting on a coat is a confusing tangle of linings and arm-holes. Sometimes coats end up on but upside down! One tried and tested method is to teach the child to lie the coat 'on its back' and kneel down at the head end. Lean forward, put your arms in the holes and flick the coat backwards over your head – making sure that no-one is behind you to be hurt by your zip. Another way is to lie the coat out in front of you, again on its back, and 'shake hands' with it. The arm you are holding with your left hand is the arm you need to put your left hand in! Zips are a matter of practice but they do seem to come more easily than laces.

Clothes lotto

A type of lotto game can be played with cards and clothes. Have a pile of cards, each with a picture of an item of clothing on it. Supply a pile of clothes

which correspond to the pictures. The game is to take turns being dealt a card, find the item of clothing that matches it from the pile and put it on. If you draw three hat cards in a row you have to try and wear all three!

The chocolate (raisins, fruit) game

An old favourite party game is the one where you roll a die and if you get a six you have to quickly put on a hat, scarf and gloves and, using a knife and fork, open a bar of chocolate and cut yourself a piece. The rest of the group are still rolling the die in turns and you must stop as soon as another person gets a six.

Another version can be to roll the die as before (alternatively, you could pass the bean bag to music and the person who is holding the bean bag when the music stops is 'it'). On getting the six the child has to put on and do up a shirt in order to earn a treat of some sort. If you do not want to use chocolate, what about raisins or fruit pieces? You can extend the children who can do shirts easily by adding gloves or shoes.

Simon says...

❑ Simon says put on your wellies.

❑ Put on your hat.

❑ Simon says put on your hat.

Each child has a pile of clothes and the aim of the game is to be dressed to go outside to play.

The clothes line race

A clothes line race may bring out the competitive spirit in someone who would not be that interested in getting dressed otherwise.

Put the items of clothing out in a line

and start the children off at one end. They must put on each item of clothing as they get to it and then race to the finish. You might like to engineer this race slightly by choosing which items of clothing you want each child to wear. Your older ones could find themselves managing buttons, zips and even laces, while the little ones will race from hats to scarves.

Managing personal hygiene

This is an activity of daily living that you will need to work on together with the parents. Toilet training is the beginning of this independence, blowing noses and washing hands and faces comes next.

Using specific activities for this skill is not particularly useful. You do need to make absolutely sure that your daily routines encourage the children to care for themselves as well as possible and that your observation programmes pick up any problems that children may be having with this.

Assessment

Stepping stones towards the goal 'dress and undress independently and manage their own hygiene'.

❑ Shows willingness to tackle problems and enjoys self-chosen challenges.

❑ Demonstrates a sense of pride in own achievement.

❑ Takes initiatives and manages developmentally appropriate tasks.

❑ Operates independently within the environment and shows confidence in linking up with others for support and guidance.

Celebrating cultures and beliefs

Why is so much made of the beliefs of other people and why do they feature so highly in the Early Learning Goal requirements? Surely children in the early years are too young to understand the meaning of most of the rituals and celebrations in familiar religions let alone the ones that they rarely come into contact with?

They are, indeed, too young to learn the theology or understand the complex belief systems that are the backbone of the festivals. But that is not why we offer children the experience of other cultures' festivals. We are hoping that by exposing them

---

Early Learning Goals

❑ Form good relationships with adults and peers.

❑ Understand that they can expect others to treat their own needs, views, cultures and beliefs with respect.

❑ Have a developing awareness of their own needs, views and feelings and be sensitive to those of others.

❑ Have a developing respect for their own cultures and beliefs and those of other peoples.

❑ Understand that people have different needs, views, cultures and beliefs, which need to be treated with respect.

❑ Respond to significant experiences showing a range of feelings when appropriate.

---

to unfamiliar practices we remove some of the fear that is the basis of future prejudice, we make the unusual interesting and we nurture a propensity to explore the beliefs of others rather than condemn them.

These festival activities are not about religion. They are about making the most of one of the richest sources of story and creative opportunity and slaying the dragons of narrow minded bias at the same time! All the opinions of others seem strange at first and empathy is a skill that can, for most children, be taught. Practising this understanding by learning about the habits of others creates a link with those other people that would not otherwise exist. This skill is not just linked to the festivals of others but to the daily habits of other families, too. Some families have cereal for breakfast, some have cereal as a bed-time snack. Children will see the difference in these habits long before they see the similarities. Continued exposure to the lives and habits of others helps the child to see the similarities sooner.

Understanding the basic beliefs of each religion helps to present the festivals in context. There are so many different subsections to so many different religions that no early years setting would be expected to understand them all. Each setting represents the culture and society in which it is based and soon becomes quite expert on the cultures of the families who attend regularly. Every group has a responsibility to be aware of and to

support the right of other people to believe in different doctrines other than their own.

Spirituality

The spirituality of young children is so difficult to describe that it fails to feature in the 'goals' approach of current practice. In our increasingly less spiritual and more materialistic world many people have forgotten how comforting a spiritual dimension in our life can be. This spirituality can transcend the confines of a particular religion. It is a spiritual experience for a small group of children to light a candle and sit quietly, thinking. It is a spiritual experience to be out in the woods in spring and to feel at one with nature or to be by the sea on a stormy day. The natural acceptance that young children have of the concept of angels, fairies and other manifestations of spiritual activity is something that is lost too readily. Nurture it - not everything needs to be explained scientifically!

Judaism

Jews believe that there is one God, a patriarchal leader, who has a special relationship with the Jews. Their holy book, the Torah, was given to Moses. Jews believe that there will be a messiah or leader sent from God to save the world. They do not believe that Jesus was the messiah. Jewish families have many specific rituals which are followed on a daily and weekly basis, many of them centred around family prayer and meal times.

Christianity

Christians, like the Jews, believe in one patriarchal God. Christians believe that Jesus Christ was the messiah and that his death saved people from damnation in that they can, if they follow the Christian path, go to heaven. Non-believers will go to hell. They believe that there will be a second coming which will mark the end of the world as we know it. Their bible is said to be the word of God. There are many different branches of Christianity, the largest of which is Catholicism.

Islam

Muslims believe in one God. His Arabic name is Allah. They believe that there have been prophets sent from God (including Noah, Abraham and Jesus). The latest of these prophets was Muhammed. Their holy book, the Qu'aran, was written before time began and dictated to Muhammed by an angel.

Hinduism

Hindus believe that God takes many different forms. They believe in re-incarnation and that God is in every object in the universe. They believe that every action has an effect on this life and the sum of these actions affects the next life – this is Karma. By learning positive Karma, a person may become freed from the cycle of reincarnations and become one with God. There are many different branches of Hinduism.

Buddhism

Buddhists follow the teachings of Siddhartha Gautama – the Buddha. Reaching nirvana (enlightenment) by learning through successive incarnations in different life forms is the aim of Buddhists. Buddha taught

of an eightfold path to enlightenment which teaches pacifist and compassionate rules for living. Meditation and quiet contemplation are hallmarks of the Buddhist faith.

Celebrating festivals

Celebrating the festivals of religions that differ from our own helps us to understand these fundamental differences and, hopefully, find some common ground where we can accept each other.

Hundreds of festivals are celebrated every year. You could not possibly cover them all and it would not be a balanced educational experience. Your aim should be to find one or two of the major festivals for each religion and celebrate them. Researching the festivals is easy enough and a rewarding study for those who wish to understand exactly what they are celebrating with the children.

The different festivals offer a wonderful array of cross-curricular opportunities. The nature of the celebration should encourage the children to accept these different beliefs as valid to their beholders. If you intend to encourage the children to celebrate this variety of cultures, you must make it clear to parents before they enroll their children. If they do not agree, they may then choose not to register the child. Removing children from certain activities is not ideal under any circumstances.

The following list suggests activities surrounding one or two of the major festivals for each religion.

Jewish Passover (Pesach)

Celebrated in the spring, this is one of the oldest festivals. Jews remember the plague sent by God to punish the Egyptians for holding the Hebrew people as slaves. They remember that the plague passed over their houses. They then celebrate the release of the

Hebrews from slavery and the journey, led by Moses, through the Red Sea to freedom.

Jews have a Seder meal at the beginning of Passover where they eat bitter food to remind them of slavery and sweet food to remind them of the sweetness of freedom.

Tasting table

Have some of the foods listed below on saucers at a tasting table. The children can taste each food and decide if it was nice or not. They then group the ones that they like best and least. Introduce the idea of bitterness and sweetness.

- ❑ Salt
- ❑ Sugar
- ❑ Lemon
- ❑ Honey
- ❑ Onion
- ❑ Grape
- ❑ Parsley
- ❑ Apple

Christian festivals

Many of the Christian festivals have incorporated older Pagan festivals into their ritual. Easter has borrowed much of its ritual from the spring fertility festival of Oestara (eggs, for example) and old Yule festivities are now incorporated into Christmas (holly, logs and candles).

As a general rule, most settings celebrate Christmas extensively and there are many craft and story ideas around for this season. Easter is a confusing festival for young children and has become an eclectic mix of eggs, bunnies and gruesome deaths. Many settings (understandably) take the soft option and select the more interesting craft activities of the season rather than attempt to tackle the complex concept of resurrection! Because Easter comes reasonably soon after Christmas, many young children have the understandably firm notion

that baby Jesus was killed. If you are going to present these Christian festivals as religious events then you should be prepared to explain the story fully and simply.

There are other Christian festivals that are not so widely celebrated that you may find less difficult to present to young children.

Saints' days

There are literally hundreds of saints days to choose from. Find out about the lives of the saints you choose to celebrate and tell the story at story time.

St Matthew – 21 September
St Mark – 25 April
St Brigid – 2 February
St Luke – 18 October
All Saints Day – 1 November

Golden gifts

Epiphany on 6 January is the last day of the 12 days of Christmas and commemorates when the wise men followed the star to the stable at Bethlehem. They brought expensive gifts of gold, frankincense and myrrh.

Wrap boxes and bottles in shiny left-over Christmas wrapping paper – ideally without snowmen or Father Christmas on. Stick on jewel shapes cut out of sticky paper and make a present pile for a baby king. Frankincense (or olibanum) is available as an aromatherapy oil and used as a rejuvenating elixir. Here it may represent resurrection but for pre-school use, the smell is an interesting start.

Muslim Ramadan

Fasting is one of the five pillars of Islam – the actions which arise out of belief. The other four are: declaration of faith, prayer, financial contribution to the community and pilgrimage. There are five main beliefs (God, the Qu'aran, the Angels, Muhammed and the prophets and the Last Day), five prayer times in a day and five categories of daily activities ranging from forbidden to obligatory.

During Ramadan in January, fasting occurs throughout the hours of

Useful books

Religions of the World edited by Professor Martin Marty Breuillly, O'Brien, Palmer (Macdonald Young Books)

World Religions series edited by W Owen Cole (Cheltenham)

The Penguin Dictionary of Religions edited by John Hinnels (Penguin)

The World's Religions N Smart (Cambridge University Press)

daylight. Children do not fast but may eat a more limited diet. Early breakfasts and the evening meal become important events.

Hungry time

Explain that during Ramadan many people do not eat in the day. Consider this just before a snack or a meal and delay the start of the meal for a few minutes while you begin to find words to describe hunger.

Hindu Divali

Lakshmi, the goddess of wealth and good fortune, is worshipped at Divali (in October/November). Lamps and candles are lit and patterns are drawn on the ground to attract her. The story of Rama and Sita, the Ramayana, is remembered. Rama, one of the representations of God, and Sita, his queen, were exiled to a forest. Sita was kidnapped, Rama rescued her and Divali celebrates this homecoming.

Divali lamps

These would be clay oil lamps (divas), often highly decorated. Using salt dough and baking it dry, make a simple flat dish. Decorate the dish and add a cardboard flame.

Mehndi patterns

Handpainting with oranges and browns of natural henna (not recommended as it is semi-permanent!) is a feature of Hindu celebrations. Traditionally, it is the girls who decorate the back of their hands with geometric designs at many major festivals and rituals.

Use water-based face paint to copy the swirls and diamonds of these intricate patterns.

Buddhism– the Birth of the Buddha

The date of this celebration varies according to regions but is usually in May. Common themes include the bathing of images of the Buddha in scented water and decorating houses.

Scented pictures

Draw simple pictures of flowers or fruit and scent them with appropriate aromatherapy oils. Orange and lemon oils are easy and safe to use and lavender or rose, although they can be expensive, make recognisable plant and flower scents.

The Hungry Ghost festival

This unusual festival in August calms unsettled spirits. Paper boats are made for the spirits to pass over into the next world and food offerings are left out for the hungry ghosts.

Paper boats

Make paper boats and decorate them and then try them out on outdoor water trays and half drain-pipe rivers. Have a rummage in the junk box and see what else would float. This is an excellent science activity.

Assessment

Stepping stones for the goal 'understand that people have different needs, views, cultures and beliefs, which need to be treated with respect'.

❑ Makes connections between different parts of their life experience.

❑ Shows a strong sense of self as a member of different communities, such as their family or setting.

❑ Has an awareness of, and shows interest and enjoyment in cultural and religious differences.

❑ Has a positive self-image and shows that they are comfortable with themselves.

Personal, Social and Emotional Development

Seasons

Seasonal celebrations and traditions

There will not be a group or class that does not mark the passage of time by looking at the changes around them as one season gives way to another. There are hundreds of wonderful ideas to mark these seasons, and the opportunity to base much early learning on the wonderful natural resource that the changing world around us offers must not be ignored.

From a Personal, Social and Emotional Development point of view, the predictability and the magic of the year full of seasons give children an unparalleled opportunity to begin to rely on the fact that some things will always happen. The understanding that seasons have always changed and that stories and rituals have grown around these changes allows the child to find her place in the world.

It is the wonder and magic, the emotions of joy and celebration, and the understanding of the value of ritual and recurring festivals that sow the seeds of spiritual strength in the children in your care, no matter how that is celebrated outwardly.

Teaching the children about other groups' festivals and practices is an excellent way to remove some of the fear and misunderstanding that can cause bias and prejudice between different religions. Focusing on what is common ground between groups is an important first step in teaching children that they do not exist in isolation from others who appear at first to be very different.

Early Learning Goals

❑ Be confident to try new activities, initiate ideas and speak in a familiar group.

❑ Form good relationships with adults and peers.

❑ Understand that they can expect others to treat their own needs, views, cultures and beliefs with respect.

❑ Work as part of a group or class, taking turns and sharing fairly, understanding that there needs to be agreed values and codes of behaviour for people, including adults and children, to work together harmoniously.

❑ Continue to be interested, excited and motivated to learn.

❑ Select and use activities and resources independently.

❑ Dress and undress independently and manage their own hygiene.

❑ Have a developing awareness of their own needs, views and feelings and be sensitive to those of others.

❑ Have a developing respect for their own cultures and beliefs and those of others.

❑ Respond to significant experiences showing a range of feelings when appropriate.

❑ Maintain attention, concentrate and sit quietly when appropriate.

Our cultural heritage

Beginning to understand other people's festivals should happen alongside a growing understanding of one's own culture and heritage. Old practices were based on the changing of the seasons. Rural people relied on their knowledge of these changes to stay alive. Their food, health and safety depended on it. It is small wonder then that high days and holidays grew around the changing of these seasons and the changes of lifestyle that accompanied them.

As you look at how the seasons change and as the children learn through observing those changes, consider another dimension – the use of these changes as a time of emotional and spiritual opportunity. The activities that are linked to these old festivals cross the boundaries of specific religions and, as a unifying practice, they are invaluable. As a link to our own past and cultural heritage, they are a wonderful and underused resource. Marking these days in a non-religious way allows the children to join together and be a part of something unique – a festival that our ancestors celebrated hundreds and hundreds of years ago. There is something reassuring about imagining these celebrations from so long ago and the learning opportunities are endless.

Feelings such as wonder and joy are hard to create artificially. Celebrations and festivals, dance, music and candlelight - these are the ways into a child's spirit and the way to nurture these precious emotions.

A year in time

Children as young as two and three are not able to remember from one year to the next – so take photos. As the child reaches three and four and is prompted by the photos of this time last year, the idea that the year is a cyclical event begins to take shape. Pictures of the nursery garden in the summer displayed in November and February are a fascinating reminder of how things were and will be again. Calendars that have all 12 months displayed at the same time help the child to see the journey through the year for what it is, one small step at a time. Disassemble an ordinary calendar with appropriate seasonal pictures and stick all 12 months, in order, onto a large board or use them as a low border in a corner of the room. Mark off each day as it passes.

Older children will enjoy watching a moon change shape throughout a month. This is an early spring or autumn activity, since in summer it is past bedtime and in winter it will be too cloudy to be successful. If you feel that the children are too young to understand how the moon changes shape, settle for the fact that they have observed that it does.

Seasons are about more than how chicks hatch and leaves fall, wonderful though those events are. There is a wealth of opportunity in every change for real Personal, Social and Emotional Development that you will not be able to teach any other way.

Solstice celebration

At four points during the year, the sun enters a different quadrant of the sky. These four dates mark the longest and the shortest day and the change-over point between the two extremes. Over centuries of observation, the ancient wise people worked out complicated astrological information using primitive recording systems and word of mouth. It is believed that Stonehenge, one of our most important ancient monuments, was built as a calendar of the movement of the sun and moon and enabled its users to predict, with accuracy, phases of the moon, lunar and solar eclipses and to measure the days between the equinoxes.

Although earth religions still value these natural events and plan ritual celebrations to mark them, the explanation of them would be too complex for young children. Understanding that there are times of the year when the day is longer than the night and vice versa and that there are days when the length of the day and night is equal (the equinoxes), is important in the marking of changes throughout the year. These dates can vary by one day each year so check a calendar if you want to be exact.

21/22 December (Midwinter, also Yule)

21/22 March (first day of spring)

21/22 June (Midsummer)

21/22 September (Harvest, first day of autumn)

May Day

This is the time of year when we really begin to enjoy spring and (slightly) better weather. May Day has been a celebration of this wonderful time of year for many centuries. The scent of spring flowers, high spirits, warm weather and the beginning of summer – the possibilities for celebration are endless.

Originally called Beltane, this was the time of year when animals were let out of the barns and fields close to home and moved to summer pastures on higher ground. Beasts were driven between two bonfires – partly as a ritual to mark the change of season and also to cleanse the animals of illness borne of a long winter in unhygienic enclosures. The wood used on the bonfires would have been chosen for its cleansing properties and herbs would have been tossed into the flames as the animals were driven between the fires.

May Day was a time of merrymaking. A young maiden would have been crowned the May Queen and, with her consort, the Green Man, she would have led the dancing. The underlying celebration of fertility mirroring the blossoming of flowers and plants formed the basis of many traditions - maypole dancing, still celebrated today, is one of them. The Beltane fires would have burned long into the night and the parties carried on until late. The herdsmen and shepherds who were to accompany the flocks to summer grazing would be spending lonely months away and May Day festivities served as a fitting send-off.

Many communities, especially more rural ones, still have fairs and fetes at this time of year and these festivities are direct descendents of these ancient May Day celebrations.

May Queen clothes and crowns

Simple white clothes would have been chosen to symbolise the purity of the maiden queen. She would have been decorated with garlands of fresh flowers and worn a wreath of greenery and flowers. Often driven through the village on the way to start the dancing and celebrations, the May Queen would have waved and smiled at her cheering and waving neighbours.

The white sheet tunics made for the angels at Christmas could be brought out again for your May Day celebrations. Find some bright coloured material for a sash and weave daisy chains to wear as jewellery. Wreaths of ivy and flowers are quite easy to make by twisting a length of ivy into a circle and pushing long stemmed flowers into the gaps in the twist. Ribbons to tie the ends in add to the effect.

There is no reason why you should not have as many different May Queens as you want. Making the boys into consorts is another simple dressing-up task – green clothes, ivy head-dresses and green face paint.

Finding an identity for the people that the children are dressing up as gives you another important dimension. Tell the girls how important the May Queen is and ask them to imagine how it would feel to be the centre of attention for the whole day. Some regal behaviour is quite appropriate. The consort would have been one of the strongest and bravest young men. The Green Man (incidentally believed to be the basis of the Robin Hood legend) represented the power of nature in human form. Allow the boys some strutting and posturing.

Parade around your hall and into your garden and playground. Either take turns to be the crowd and the procession or imagine the crowd. End the parade either at the maypole, if you are going on to further May Day celebrations, or at an appropriately extravagant snack time!

Maypoles

Tall poles with coloured ribbons hung from beneath a wreath of greenery set in the village green, maypoles were the centre of exuberant fairs and fetes.

Led by the May Queen, the dancers wove in and out of each other, creating

complex patterns with the ribbons. As the ribbons formed the pattern, the wreath would slide down the pole and the dancers would find themselves nearer and nearer the centre.

Maypole dancing is too complicated for pre-school children. This does not mean that you have to abandon the whole idea, though. Weaving in and out of each other is possible and it would create a simple pattern that the children could see and enjoy.

Stick a fairly tall pole firmly in the grass and pin six different coloured lengths of ribbon to the top. Leave yourself a long length of ribbon (a two-metre pole could easily accommodate six-metre lengths of ribbon).

Make a circle of six children in fancy dress, each holding the end of the ribbon, and encourage them to move around the pole, weaving in and out of each other, every other child going one way and the other three the other way. You may want to practise the weaving without the ribbons, making the children move in the right direction and at an appropriate speed. Then give the children the ribbons and they will see the pattern they are making forming above them around the maypole. This simple in-and-out pattern is easy enough to undo and start again with a different set of dancers.

Give the spectators percussion instruments, bells and drums, or encourage them to clap to accompany the music you have chosen to dance to.

Other activities could be added to your May Day celebrations following the theme. Simple ideas based on the following headings would be appropriate:

❑ Flower arrangements;

❑ Parties and fairs;

❑ Bonfires;

❑ Scent herbs and flowers.

Midsummer

'The iron tongue of midnight hath told twelve
Lovers, to bed; 'tis almost fairy time'.

(*A Midsummer Night's Dream*, Act 1 Scene 5)

Long warm days and fairy-filled nights - Midsummer really could be magic! There are a vast number of midsummer themes that you could choose to mark this time.

To a certain extent, you will be limited by your geography and resources. City centre children will have more difficulty than country dwellers marking these old country festivities but any believer in fairies will know that they can live quite happily in the city, too…

Fairies

Fairy stories, fairy cakes, fairy footsteps, fairies at the bottom of the garden - no childhood is complete without at least an introduction to the world of fairies. Some children might dismiss the idea but others will find the idea as enchanting as many adults still do. Midsummer Eve night is, traditionally, the time when fairies meet in the forests to dance the midsummer ball. Fairies tell stories, have feasts, wear beautiful clothes, dance and sing and tell jokes. They can fly wherever they want to go and can be invisible if they need to be.

Fairy ball

Using net and strips of ribbon and lace or, more extravagantly, wire and net wings, the children can dress up cheaply. Traditionally, fairies can be of either sex but some boys will probably be unwilling to try this role out. There are other fairy folk that they could be interested in – pixies and elves, for example. For this celebration, I suggest that you have an adult Fairy Queen rather than a child May Queen. This person can then lead the storytelling (fairy stories, of course!) and dancing for which you will find suitable fairy music in most music shops.

The food for the feast should be cut small and be delicately decorated. The children can make the food themselves:

❑ Small sandwiches on a plate decorated with daisies;

❑ Fresh fruit punch;

❑ Honey biscuits – made small;

❑ Tiny iced fairy cakes.

Midsummer flowers

Crops, flowers and plants are at their most beautiful at this time of year and this is a season of abundance and beauty. Plant wildflower seeds in decorated pots in time for midsummer and make pipe-cleaner fairies with gauze skirts and ribbon hair to sit in amongst the flowers. Some of the easiest to grow flowers can also be put to good use.

❑ Marigolds are believed to be a natural pest control – plant them in pots to put at windows and doors;

❑ Violets will be in bloom and can be candied for cake decorations;

❑ Nasturtium flowers are edible and add colour to salads.

Harvest time

By now we have almost forgotten what it is like to be really cold and wet on a winter's day. We are used to our gardens and countryside being green and beautiful and the flowers have borne fruit. In the past, this was the most important time of the year for many communities. Storing and saving the food harvested would mean enough to eat for the rest of the year. This was the one time of year when there really was enough food to go around. Eating well now would protect people through the harshness of the winter, storing up the goodness in their bodies. It was a time of hard work and whole communities would pull together to gather the crops and pick the fruits.

When the work was done and the food in and safe from the less predictable weather of October and November, there was good reason for a feast of fresh food. Harvest is entirely about food. It is about the results of hard work and favourable conditions and the combined efforts of a whole community.

Harvest lunch

Having a harvest feast is an ideal time to invite parents, friends and siblings into the group. Each guest could bring a contribution of a savoury or sweet dish. Fresh ingredients are the order of the day, if at all possible.

Set a large long table with white tablecloths (or sheets) and decorate it with ivy and sheaves of corn (or dried grasses if easier to come by), put jugs of flowers on the table and encourage your own community to enjoy a lovely lunch together.

This will reap rewards in many ways:

❑ Promoting the eating of fresh and healthy food;

❑ Enabling families to meet each other;

❑ Giving you the opportunity to see parents and children together;

❑ Remembering how to have fun in a simple, easy-to-organise way;

❑ Celebrating in the same way people have done for centuries;

❑ Giving parents the opportunity to talk to you in a relaxed atmosphere;

❑ Giving you the opportunity to have an open day and explain your plans for the year ahead;

❑ Making new friends and welcoming new parents into the group.

Preserving fruits and vegetables

Making food last throughout the year was the basis of the housewife or cook's art. There were no freezers, cans or packers, so people had to eat food in season. Meat would have been salted or dried, fruit and vegetables would have been preserved or pickled.

Jams, jellies, mincemeat, chutneys and pickles are easy enough to make and recipes are readily available. Getting the children to chop the softer

① Fold straw for head and body.
② Tie neck ⓐ and waist ⓑ.

③ Push straw through for arms.
④ Tie crossover ⓒ string to keep arms secure.
⑤ Push daisies in for eyes.

ingredients with safe table knives, and smell the different smells is a great experience. Scent is an important sense in the formation of good memories and activities like these will be sealed in the child's subconscious for ever. Making it a positive, fun time, is, therefore, doubly important.

Make jars for Christmas presents or have a table sale at the end of one of the sessions to raise money for funds. Decorating circles of paper for the top of the jars is an absorbing task. You can also choose circles of fabric to cover the jar top. Label the jars, too, and you have covered measuring, recognising words, fine motor skills and early science to name but a few skills!

Corn dollies

Corn dollies were made for many reasons. They were toys, good luck charms and complex creations became valued gifts. Getting hold of corn stalks may not be easy but straw is readily available in pet shops. Find a small handful of long stalks and fold it in half. The loop is the head and the two ends are the two legs. Tie the bundle with string where the waist should be. Take a shorter length of straw, bind it in the middle so that it stays together and thread it through the folded bunch, above the waist, for arms. Tie the arms in securely with string or twine.

These dolls can be decorated with simple cotton skirts and shawls. Small dried flowers look good around the head.

Healthy eating

While food is such a focus of attention, take the time to look at good things to eat and introduce the idea of healthy eating.

We all know that smoking is a bad idea and that we must clean our teeth and not eat too many sweets, but we should bear in mind that the children we are working with are very young and cannot possibly have any control over the food that is brought into their home or the habits of the adults around them. Teaching by example is by far the best way to encourage healthy habits and, as part and parcel of the nurturing of self-esteem, caring for one's own health is an important habit to learn.

Most foods are not harmful if eaten in moderation. Teach the children to enjoy fresh food, its preparation, its taste, the variety available and the knowledge about where the food comes from. Tell the children how good the food you are offering them is and how important good food is for health. Be positive, don't focus on what might happen if the child eats the wrong thing but on how enjoyable good food is. Make sure you give the children good food at snack time and that the parents of the children in your group have access to advice if they should want it.

Yule

There is no shortage of ideas for crafts and celebrations at this time of year, but understanding that the rituals we observe have roots in far older ceremonies may well give more meaning to the rather shallow commercial face that Christmas has perhaps shown recently. Pre-Christian religions celebrated the handing over of power from the Holly King to the Oak King and the rebirth of the Sun God. Parallels with Father Christmas and the Christian Christmas story are easy to make.

Before Christmas became the festival of choice in the middle of the winter, there were always festivals of light of one sort or another to break the terrible monotony and hardship of ancient winters. The December solstice marks the longest night when the days are as short as they can be and the nights as long as they will get.

Yule was a time of staying in by a warm fire and telling tales. The Yule log we still have in our modern celebrations was, in days gone by, the largest log (traditionally birch) that could be fitted into the hearth and kept burning for the 12 days of Yule. A branch of a tree was decorated as part of the festival preparation and candles were burnt throughout the long evenings to light the proceedings. Food saved from harvest was eaten and this time of darkness and cold was made easier to bear by the celebration of the promise of easier times just around the corner.

The timing of Yule, around 21 December, fits in with many end-of-term dates and is a fitting date to celebrate this magical season as a group.

Yule logs

Decorating a log with ribbons, snow made from soap flakes (these may irritate sensitive skins, so beware), holly and ivy is still a common custom. These are cheap and easy to make. If you decide to drill a hole and add a candle, you should make sure that the adult who takes the child home with the log is aware of how great a fire risk this is.

You could have a large decorated log in your setting over this period and light candles (non-drip church candles on a high shelf out of reach) to represent the flames burning.

Decorating chocolate swiss rolls with chocolate butter cream and holly is another great favourite.

Candles

Candles are fascinating and beautiful – but so dangerous! Supervise even the oldest and most trustworthy of your children at all times if you decide to look at candles.

You could have a candle-lighting time at circle time during this dark time of year and teach the children to just sit quietly and enjoy the flickering of the flames. You could light one candle a day for the last 12 days of term. Paint plain candles, stick sequins or tiny beads on with melted wax that will melt and drop the decoration before it burns and send home as Christmas gifts (with the obligatory fire risk warning, of course). Make candles out of cardboard rolls by covering them in paper and adding a cardboard flame to the top of the tube. An Advent calendar made out of these cardboard candles is effective - simply add another candle to the Advent display each day.

Assessment

Stepping stones for the goal 'have a developing respect for their own cultures and beliefs and those of others'.

❑ Separates from main carer with support.

❑ Separates from main carer with confidence.

❑ Has a sense of belonging.

❑ Shows care and concern for self.

❑ Talks freely about their home and community.

❑ Has a sense of self as a member of different communities.

❑ Expresses needs and feelings in appropriate ways.

❑ Initiates interactions with other people.

Personal, Social and **Emotional Development**

THEME

Water

Working together with water

The children will have seen images of drought-ridden communities on the television and in the papers, but they are too young to understand much more than the fact that some countries do not get enough rain.

Some children may have experienced the mild water shortage we suffer from in dry summers here. Conserving water becomes a household way of life in these times and the children catch on quickly. Take a photo of your dry lawn and dusty flower beds on a hot, dry summer's day and then, in February, when it seems to have been raining for ever, take it out and have a look. The children will enjoy the comparison.

Understanding how water affects other communities in the world is an interesting discussion point. Boat people, river dwellers, societies in the frozen north and desert families all make for useful mini topics on a water theme. Imagining what life is like for others is not easy for children of this age but, encouraged, they can begin to understand that life can be different elsewhere. Empathy is hard to teach but if you regularly, openly, empathise, the children will follow suit.

Learning about the cycle of water, from cloud to rain to stream, river and sea and back again is only really suitable for the older children but there are ways of introducing the beginnings of this understanding - the idea that water flows. This is where that great staple, the water tray, comes in. Playing with

Early Learning Goals

❑ Form good relationships with adults and peers.

❑ Work as part of a group or class, taking turns and sharing fairly, understanding that there needs to be agreed values, and codes of behaviour for groups of people, including adults and children, to work together harmoniously.

❑ Select and use activities and resources independently.

❑ Understand what is right and wrong and why.

water guides children towards some of the goals in each area of learning. Playing together in the water tray is a realistic way of teaching cooperation, respect for each other, turn-taking and sharing resources.

The cooperation and commitment required to put out house fires when a chain of people passing buckets from the village pond to the burning house was the only hope is humbling. The ferocity of the arguments over water-rich lands is understandable. Sharing water is a basic human activity.

The water chain

Outdoors, on a warm day, line the children up a few steps apart from each other on marked spots. Give each child a plastic jug and pour water into the first jug. The children then pour water into their neighbours' jugs and

go back to their place. Leave a gap of two or three children and pour more water into the first jug.

As well as being good fun, this is an activity that requires care not to spill the water and encouragement from one child to another. Watching the water make its way down the line is surprisingly satisfying.

The production line

In a water tray, set up a system whereby water has to be poured, guided, sieved, turned and sprinkled in a certain order. One child pours the water from a jug through a funnel into a bucket held by another child which he then pours through a sieve onto a channel which guides it into the final bucket, held by another child who then pours it back into the first jug.

There's a hole in my bucket

You will need an old damaged bucket, a garden, a warm day and children who do not mind getting their feet wet. Fill the leaky bucket with water and ask one child to take the water across the garden to another child. The other child then carries the water back to another child, and so on, until the water has all leaked out. The aim of the game is to give as many children as possible a turn at carrying the bucket.

The juice bar

Set up a stall, ideally outside (but not necessarily if you have wipeable floors) and give the stall keeper jugs of water coloured with a few drops of food colouring and plastic cups. The other children can buy 'flavoured juice' at the stall. You could add ice cubes, slices of orange and straws to make the drink more interesting.

Sprays and umbrellas

This is definitely a hot day idea. Set up a garden sprinkler and, with the children in pairs, give them an umbrella to share to run through the spray with. They should take it in turns to hold the umbrella. If it's on grass, take care as it will be slippy.

Sunken treasure

Put glass beads in the water tray. Adding bubbles to the water makes it harder to find the treasure. Provide sieves for the children to find the treasure with and boxes to store the treasure in. The children should aim to all have the same number of beads at the end of the game.

Water fighting

There is nothing that the children enjoy more on a hot day than throwing water at each other. Many groups shy away from this sort of horse play, believing it to be aggressive and not acceptable. Children do, however, need to learn how to manage their energy and this 'stage fighting' teaches several valuable social skills. Kindlon and Thompson in *Raising Cain - Protecting the Emotional Life of Boys* (Michael Joseph) argue that allowing boys to learn to play by rules like this teaches them to manage their natural tendency

to rough and tumble and that by avoiding all rough games we are not allowing them to develop their characters fully. We have to allow the natural exuberance that many children have, especially boys, to be as valid a form of expression as chatting is to others.

Rules are important for all games. It is in situations like this that they are most obviously essential. You should only give the children small containers for the water. Fromage frais pots are ideal because they are unlikely to do any damage if they are thrown.

Be prepared to referee, giving a child 'time out' if he breaks any of the rules but allowing him back in to carry on and prove that he has learned his lesson. You should have a safe zone within the boundaries and the boundaries should be clearly marked.

Children should not be made to join in this rough and tumble but do encourage everyone to have a go. Getting wet is not the end of the world and playing together in this way is fun and educational. If you are joining in as well, you will encourage the more reticent. Your rules might be something like this:

❑ No throwing pots or anything other than water;

❑ No playing outside the boundary;

❑ No banging into anyone else or hurting them;

❑ No wetting anyone who is in the safe zone;

❑ No unkind words;

❑ Stop immediately if a whistle goes, it might mean someone has slipped and a grown-up has to see to it.

Your sanctions will be removal from the game for a certain amount of time.

Assessment

Stepping stones towards the goal 'work as part of a group or class, taking turns and sharing fairly, understanding that there needs to be agreed values, and codes of behaviour for groups of people, including adults and children, to work together harmoniously'.

❑ Feels safe and secure and demonstrates a sense of trust.

❑ Seeks out others to share experiences.

❑ Relates and makes attachments to members of their group.

❑ Demonstrates flexibility and adapts their behaviour to different events, social situations and changes in routine.

❑ Values and contributes to own well-being and self control.

Personal, Social and Emotional Development

Colour

Colours of the world

Colour recognition is so much a part of daily conversation in early years settings that the theme of colours could be said to be an ongoing one. Every time you ask a child which colour cup they want, to pass a red brick, to draw or paint and then discuss the picture, you are teaching colour recognition. The good feeling that comes with knowing something and getting it right is a boost to confidence and self-esteem. Colour recognition is a basic skill and one which young children in the Foundation Stage will soon experience consistent success at.

Skin tone

So much is made of the colour of people's skin. Bias and prejudice, cruelty and favouritism, the colour of one's skin has counted for much and caused some terrible suffering. How we teach the children in our care to move on from this bigotry and to learn to accept others for who they are and not how they look is important.

Early Learning Goals

❑ Form good relationships with adults and peers.

❑ Understand that they can expect others to treat their own needs, views, cultures and beliefs with respect.

❑ Continue to be interested, excited and motivated to learn.

❑ Select and use activities and resources independently.

❑ Have a developing respect for their own cultures and beliefs and those of other people.

There are crayons and paints available now which come in packs of skin tones. You will see that they are all shades of brown and it is an interesting task to match a colour with each child's skin tone. Don't be afraid of this. Prejudice is the belief that one colour is more or less valued than another. If you are teaching your children that we are all shades of the same colour and suggesting that they match their own skin to the crayons or paints available, you are positively reinforcing the child's understanding of himself and his peers. Once a point has been made and the children have examined the colours in the faces around them, they will move on to something new, hopefully taking a basic understanding that all skins come from the same colour range.

During the summer, point out to the lighter children that their skin changes colour to cope with the bright sun – a sun tan. Taking two photos – a 'before sun exposure' and an 'after sun exposure' – is entertaining and educational.

Some races usually have dark hair and some usually have light. Some have blue eyes and some do not. There is really little difference other than that. Facial features make groups of people look similar in the same way that members of a family look alike. Stress the normality of this. Instilling this basic acceptance of other people into young children is really important for their own future ability to deal with the prejudice that they will undoubtedly encounter around them.

When painting faces or people always have the skin colours available. If a child chooses green or blue for a face, that's fine! If they want to choose a dark, dark brown for another face, that's fine too. Don't interfere. Let them experiment. Providing that your attitude is inclusive and accepting, your children will not begin life with a

prejudice that will prevent them from seeing the world as it really is. Now and again, you might want them to do a representational drawing of themselves or their family or friends and you could help them to choose the right colour for the skin on such an occasion.

Feeling blue?

We use colours to represent our mood in ordinary conversations:

❑ Seeing red;

❑ Feeling blue;

❑ A grey day;

❑ Yellow belly coward;

❑ Green with envy;

❑ White with fright;

❑ A red letter day.

Other colours are said to represent feelings:

❑ Purple for passion;

❑ Pink for love;

❑ White for purity;

❑ Green is said to be a calming colour;

❑ Yellow is an energising colour;

❑ Blue is cold;

❑ Red is hot.

Children are often as aware of the nature of the effect of colour on us as adults. This knowledge has leaked into our language and phraseology. If you ask a child to find an angry colour, she will come up with a series of colours, predominantly reds and oranges or black. Cold colours are blues, whites and pale yellows and greens.

Painting feelings

Art therapists have long used art as a medium for expressing emotions and feelings that are hard to express with words. This is a skill that takes a great deal of training and it would be inappropriate for you to begin this sort of work with a child but it might be possible to do some preventative work and begin to examine emotions as well.

Discuss an emotion: how you might get to feel that way, how the emotion itself feels, and how it looks to others. Talk about which colours you would choose to paint such a feeling, then paint it. Write the emotion on the painting and display them all together. If you have an artist on the staff, a simple black marker outline drawing of a face showing the relevant expression looks good on top of the child's collection of colours.

Anger, sadness, joy, fear, jealousy, love and worry are all basic feelings that the children will have already experienced and will understand.

War paint

Tribes - from the Celts in the north to Aborigines in the south - have used coloured paint on their faces to make them look ferocious. The use of natural plant and flower dyes meant that the painting process could take days of ritual preparation - also because the frame of mind required to face such terrible battles would have taken a long time to acquire!

Children love face painting. Collect pictures of faces painted for war and festivals and copy some of the designs onto the children's faces. Water-based face paint applied with a thin brush is by far the most effective.

When you have your warriors ready, line them up in two rows facing each other and allow them to make intimidating growls and gestures at each other to see how it might have felt.

War dances were part religious ritual, part self-hypnosis and part intimidatory. A Maori Haka (such as that performed by the All Blacks rugby team prior to a match) is fun to attempt. No one will mind if you make up a few steps but if you know a New Zealander who can teach you the real thing, even better.

Totem poles

It is a misconception that totem poles were worshipped by native Americans. Whilst some of them may have been used by the medicine men or shamans of a group to focus the mind during

growl.. growl!   scary.. scary..!

meditation, totem poles were predominantly used to mark territory for family groups or to tell stories of adventures in a society which did not keep written records.

A fence post, either round or halved (longways) makes a perfect totem pole. Paint the pole with gloss paint and then let the children decorate it with poster paint to mark out where their garden is or to tell the story of a trip or adventure that you have had as a group. When the children's paint has dried, varnish the totem pole with yacht varnish and stick it in the earth in your garden.

Recording important events in this imaginative way helps children remember them and learn from them, too. Choose the colours you use with care and encourage the children to name the colours that they use. Don't be too specific about what they paint but do let them discuss with you what they are portraying as they go.

South American worry dolls

These tiny brightly coloured, roughly made dolls are often found in craft shops, fair trade stalls and Oxfam shops. The idea is that you tell these little dolls your worries and, on the basis that a problem shared is a problem halved, your worry will fade!

Different cultures are the source of some wonderful art and craft opportunities. Ecuadorian dolls are typically dressed in stripy cloaks or ponchos and the rich colours that these dolls are made of reflect something of the vibrant culture of South America - the reds and purples and blues and violets are pleasing. Making worry dolls is not as difficult as it seems.

The dolls that you can buy are often made up into headbands and brooches and are small - too small for young children to manage. Old-fashioned

wooden clothes pegs (dolly pegs), however, are easily dressed up, large enough to handle and a similar shape to the worry dolls.

Find some suitable fabric (woven wool in multi colours) and cut it into a rectangle, about 6 x 4 cm. Cut from the centre of one of the short sides to the centre of the cloth and slip it onto the wooden peg to form a 'cloak'. Tie a belt of twisted wool around the waist of the doll and knot it firmly. Paint a face on the peg with felt pen and either stick black wool on for hair and plait it, or glue a triangle of material on for a headscarf.

When each child in the group has a doll, explain what worry dolls are and that some people believe that telling the dolls a worry at night will help ease the problem by morning. You may find that you begin an interesting discussion about worrying. Even very young children worry quite seriously about lots of things. Many of their worries are easy to explain away but some seem quite unfathomable. No untrained person should even try to counsel these very young children and that is not the aim of this group. Your intention should be merely to acknowledge that worries are real, that they differ from person to person and that it often helps to tell someone you trust about the worry.

Extension ideas

You may well find, especially with older children, that you strike a cord with these dolls.

❑ Younger children will probably enjoy seeing the toy emerge and playing with the doll in a group with the other children afterwards. Making the doll walk and talk is absorbing and valuable play experience for even the very youngest in your group.

❑ You will also have met some interesting colours along the way that

your older children will be ready to learn about. Looking at how the colours go together will let you look at the mixing of blues and reds to make purples, you will meet violet and indigo as well and the shades of red will enable you to introduce the idea of dark and light colours.

❑ Look at woven cloths and have a go at making stripy fabric on a loom. It is easy to build a wooden frame and use wool to make a square of fabric. Choose wool that reminds you of the colours that you met in the worry doll activity.

Assessment

Stepping stones towards the goal 'form good relationships with peers'.

❑ Feels safe and secure and demonstrates a sense of trust.

❑ Seeks out others to share experiences.

❑ Relates and make attachments to members of their group.

❑ Demonstrates flexibility and adapts their behaviour to different events, social situations and changes in routine.

❑ Values and contributes to own well-being and self control.

All about me

Special days

Children under eight are still forming their characters and personalities and these early years experiences are crucial. A child who believes that they are 'no good' will soon cease to try and the prophesy is soon, sadly, self-fulfilling.

Do we spend enough time telling the children in our care how much we appreciate them? Especially those who are in extended care situations? In a family, a child is likely to be hugged and kissed and praised for little successes through that astonishing gift we are handed along with the new - born – parental love. Even seemingly unlovable little monsters are the apples of their parents' eyes.

As carers of very young children, don't forget to nurture the child's budding self-confidence. The best way to do this is to do it all the time, in all of your

dealings with them and in all of your conversations. Your activities should be planned with all of their needs in mind, including the requirement that their environment should foster self-confidence and self-esteem. This is the only way to successfully support young children away from parents.

One easy activity to set up is the special day. Each child has a day on which the group concentrates, just for a short time, on the skills and gifts that child brings to the group.

During a circle time, the leader could inform the group that today is Jane's special day. The leader will start the ball rolling by saying why she enjoys Jane's company. The children will be encouraged to join in and describe their positive feelings for Jane. Some special work, a picture or a model that Jane has made can go on the 'special day tray' along with the 'special day certificate' that confirms how kind, funny, considerate or imaginative Jane is and maybe a note from Jane's family giving their support.

This process should not take longer than a few minutes and is not intended to make poor Jane curl up with embarrassment, so handle it sensitively and make sure that you are prepared with valid comments. Children will see through false compliments, making the activity counter-productive. If you really can't find a good point, delay that child's special day for a while and spend some time observing and assessing what is going wrong.

Be careful what you praise. Praise

enthusiasm, exuberance, exploration, humour, questioning and challenging as well as the easier docile and quiet behaviour. Do not fall into the trap of praising girls for quiet, good behaviour and boys for assertive, exploratory behaviour – it is surprisingly easy to do. Don't be afraid to praise children for being clever; there is nothing wrong with it, just keep a balance and praise a child who is less clever for his skills too, with the same enthusiasm.

Use something like the certificate (see right) and letter to involve parents and make sure that you send all special day paperwork home – parents need praise too!

Early Learning Goals

❑ Form good relationships with adults and peers.

❑ Understand that they can expect others to treat their own needs, views, cultures and beliefs with respect.

❑ Have a developing awareness of their own needs, views and feelings and be sensitive to those of others.

❑ Consider the consequences of words and actions for themselves and others.

❑ Maintain attention, concentrate and sit quietly when appropriate.

The certificate has been left blank for you to copy and fill in. The wording might say something like:
'This special day certificate has been awarded to Jane Smith on the 1st July 2000. Jane's friends and teachers like her so much because she is kind to other children. She can make them laugh with her funny stories and she can ask interesting questions.

Well done Jane!

Example letter for parents

Dear Parents,

Once during each term we have a special day for each child. On this day we celebrate that child's strengths and let them know how important they are to us all!
The special day tray will have the child's name, some work that they have chosen to go on the tray and a certificate that records what was said at 'special day time' about that child during our group conversation. Your child will bring the certificate home.

Your child's special day is on _____
Please could you complete the sentence below to add to the value of this important day for your child. We will read it out at group time.

(child's name) is loved by us because _____

Special Day Certificate

Personal, Social and Emotional Development

People who help us

Families

Children learn from their families about coping with certain situations. They know, by the age of three, that the adults in the house are in charge and will keep them safe. They watch parents rush to turn down a boiling-over pan, change fuses and fix things, give medicine to make them feel better and provide security in the middle of the night. Siblings are important playmates and grandparents often provide a safe haven.

Including the family in the list of people who help us is important. Successful families, like all good teams, have different roles for different members and all the roles work together, usually fairly harmoniously. The children will have an intrinsic understanding of this even by the age of three and may well be able to tell you something about each family member.

As more and more children are living in extended and blended family

groups, you will have to have done your research before you begin this project. Sending a letter home requesting extra information is a good idea. It gives families the opportunity to speak to you about awkward or new situations so that you do not find yourself making involuntary mistakes.

Your family tree will not be a dry document. Include whatever you think will make it more interesting. You will probably want to make it a family folder for ease of presentation. You may include:

❑ Photos of the child and of the members of the family;

❑ Paintings;

❑ Descriptions;

❑ Diagrams of relationships;

❑ Mementos;

❑ Memories of specific family occasions as told by the child and transcribed by you.

Here is an example of a letter you could write to parents:

Dear Parents,

Our Family Tree Project:

We are planning a project that will result in each child making a family tree.

Some children will be concentrating on immediate family, that is parents and siblings

and possibly grandparents. Other groups will include aunts, uncles and cousins and possibly great grandparents.

We need as much information as possible to make this a useful learning experience for your child. Please fill in the attached questionnaire as fully as possible. Photos of the people included in the tree would be really helpful. The document will come home when finished so all photos will come back to you.

If you live in a blended family, please give us details of the people whom your child considers to be his or her family, whether or not they are officially related. If your child does not see or know one of his or her parents, please just leave the appropriate section blank. The top line of each box is filled in as an example. If a close relative is no longer living, please indicate so on the form.

If there is any information that you want us to have before we begin this project, please contact us. It is important that we get the details of your family correct, otherwise the family tree will not be as useful a project as we would like it to be.

As always, we appreciate your help and hope that you will enjoy the results of this interesting project!

Yours sincerely

When you have collected what you think is enough information you can

---

Early Learning Goals

❑ Form good relationships with adults and peers.

❑ Understand that they can expect others to treat their own needs, views, cultures and beliefs with respect.

❑ Have a developing awareness of their own needs, views and feelings and those of others.

❑ Maintain attention, sit quietly and concentrate when appropriate.

begin. Using words alone is not enough. With the child, look at the information you have and ask them to tell you something about the person you are discussing. You will be able to prompt the child by using some of the information supplied by the family. Some children will provide ample details on their own. Ideally, the child will think of something positive about each family member, along the theme of 'People who help us'. On a new sheet of paper for each relative, write down neatly and clearly what the child says. Write only two or three sentences - and keep them polite. Although the children may well say something funny about Grandad, remember that words

it being drawn out, with the names of their important people on. This is a long task and one which you need time to do properly. If you do not want to put the usual tree shape on, then rename the file something like 'My family book'.

When you have finished the book, make time to sit and browse through it with the child, talking about the people and the pictures. They will enjoy this important pre-reading activity. Encourage the children to share their family files with each other,

keep an ear on the conversations that are taking place and if a child is

child and the relationship you have with the family as well as the child herself. Some children want to talk about changes and others don't. Divorce and remarriage can shape families into new units and the child may find that a family tree project is the last thing she wants to do! On the other hand, some children may find that going over changes on paper really helps them to solidify these new situations in their minds.

Bereavement leaves a large hole in anyone's life. The loss of a close relative such as a loved grandparent is traumatic for anyone, the loss of a parent to a young child is, understandably, devastating. You may well be involved in separate projects to help the child come to terms with this loss and you may feel that a family tree would not help. You may decide that to include memories and comments about a recently deceased relative would be helpful. Discuss this with the family and your other advisers until you are sure that you have made the right decision.

Family details for the family tree project						
Name	**Relationship**	**Skills or hobbies**	**Known as** (to the child)			**Photo sent**
Parents or adults with parental responsibility						
Jane Smith	Mother	Singing and dancing	Mummy			Yes
Grandparents						
Phyllis Jones	stepfather's mother	Painting	Nanny			Yes
Aunts and uncles (known to the child)						
Betty Smith	Mother's sister	Karaoke	Aunty Bets			No
Siblings (please include step or half siblings if known to the child)						
Emily Brown	Half sister	Brownies	Living with child	Yes	Age 7	Yes
Cousins (known to the child)						
William Smith	Betty's son	Motocross	Billy		Age 13	Yes

on paper soon look more insulting than they were meant to! Add the photo if supplied or a drawing done by the child.

You will soon have quite a sheaf of documents. Collate all the papers into a file and on the front cover, draw a simple line diagram to show the relationship of each person to the child. This is too difficult for most pre-schoolers to do but they will love to see

finding it hard to accept the set-up of another's perhaps more complex family, step in and help the child to explain who is in his family. The other child will learn to accept differences as simply different and not 'weird'.

Family changes

A child who has recently undergone major family changes may well not be ready for this project. It will depend on the ability of the family to support the

Personal, Social
and Emotional Development

Planning for Personal, Social and Emotional Development

These pages explain how the 15 activities in this book cover all the Early Learning Goals for Personal, Social and Emotional Development.

The Early Learning Goals for Personal, Social and Emotional Development

PS 1 Be confident to try new activities, initiate ideas and speak in a familiar group.

PS 2 Form good relationships with adults and peers.

PS 3 Understand that they can expect others to treat their own needs, views, cultures and beliefs with respect.

PS 4 Work as part of a group or class, taking turns and sharing fairly, understanding that there needs to be agreed values and codes of behaviour for groups of people, including adults and children, to work together harmoniously.

PS 5 Continue to be interested, excited and motivated to learn.

PS 6 Select and use activities and resources independently.

PS 7 Dress and undress independently and manage their own personal hygiene.

PS 8 Have a developing awareness of their own needs, views and feelings and be sensitive to the needs, views and feelings of others.

PS 9 Have a developing respect for their own cultures and beliefs and those of other people.

PS 10 Understand that people have different needs, views, cultures and beliefs, which need to be treated with respect.

PS 11 Understand what is right what is wrong and why.

PS 12 Consider the consequences of words and actions for themselves and others.

PS 13 Respond to significant experiences showing a range of feelings when appropriate.

PS 14 Maintain attention, concentrate and sit quietly when appropriate.

● ● ● ● ● ● ● ● ● ● ● ● ●

Circle time (pages 18-21)

Stepping stones towards the goal 'understand what is right and wrong and why' are detailed here. Ideas for discussion, routine and problem-solving are included.

Related goals: 1, 2, 3, 4, 5, 8, 11, 12, 14

● ● ● ● ● ● ● ● ● ● ● ● ●

Choosing time (pages 22-23)

This activity concentrates on how to make the most of an important aspect of the pre-school curriculum. The stepping stones leading to the goal 'select and use activities and resources independently' are looked at in more detail. Planning tips and ideas are included.

Related goals: 1, 2, 3, 4, 6

● ● ● ● ● ● ● ● ● ● ● ● ●

The home corner (pages 24-29)

Ideas for the extension of this valuable early years experience are given with suggestions for resources. Stepping stones for the goal 'have a developing awareness of their own needs, views and feelings and be sensitive to the needs, views and feelings of others' are highlighted.

Related goals: 1, 2, 3, 4, 6, 7, 8, 9, 12

● ● ● ● ● ● ● ● ● ● ● ● ●

Learning to share (pages 30-31)

Games and ideas to encourage children to begin to share. Stepping stones towards the goal 'consider the consequences of words and actions for themselves and others' are given.

Related goals: 2, 3, 4, 9, 10, 11, 12

● ● ● ● ● ● ● ● ● ● ● ● ●

Wait for it! (pages 32-33)

The perennial problem of waiting patiently is covered. Games and discussion ideas to enable children to begin to realise the importance of waiting are included along with stepping stones towards the goal 'maintain attention, concentrate and sit quietly when appropriate'.

Related goals: 2, 4, 8, 12, 14

Facing up to fears (pages 34-35)

A look at fear and bravery with suggestions for approaches to some common insecurities. An important step on the road to self-confidence. Stepping stones towards the goal 'continue to be interested, excited and motivated to learn' are included.

Related goals: 1, 5, 6, 9, 13

Mirror faces (pages 36-37)

Activities for the introduction of the vocabulary required for children to begin to express their own feelings and recognise emotions in themselves and others. Stepping stones towards the goal 'respond to significant experiences showing a range of feelings when appropriate' are given.

Related goals: 12, 13, 14

Travelling Tara (pages 38-39)

A wide-ranging ongoing project idea that covers several PSED and literacy goals. Parental involvement forms an important part of this activity. Stepping stones towards the goal 'be confident to try new activities, initiate ideas and speak in a familiar group' are included.

Related goals: 1, 2, 3, 4, 9, 10

Dressing games (pages 40-41)

The concept of independence is discussed alongside ideas for encouraging children to dress and begin to care for themselves. Stepping stones leading to the goal 'dress and undress independently and manage their own personal hygiene' are given.

Related goals: 5, 7, 14

Celebrating cultures and beliefs (pages 42-45)

A closer look at the practices of major world religions. Activity ideas for some well-known and less well-known festivals are included. Stepping stones for the goal 'understand that people have different needs, views, cultures and beliefs, which need to be treated with respect' are included.

Related goals: 2, 3, 8, 9, 10, 13

Seasons: Seasonal celebrations and traditions (pages 46-51)

A wide-ranging series of ideas looking at the changing year based on old local traditions. Stepping stones for the goal 'have a developing respect for their own cultures and beliefs and those of other people' are included.

Related goals: 1, 2, 3, 4, 5, 6, 7, 8, 9, 13, 14

Water: Working together with water (pages 52-53)

Cooperation and team work sit comfortably with early science in this close look at the value of water play in PSED. Stepping stones for the goal 'work as part of a group or class, taking turns and sharing fairly, understanding

that there needs to be agreed values and codes of behaviour for groups of people, including adults and children, to work together harmoniously' are given.

Related goals: 2, 4, 6, 11

Colour: Colours of the world (pages 54-57)

A frank look at skin colour and acceptance of others, with suggestions for raising this subject in single or mixed culture groups. Stepping stones for the goal 'form good relationships with adults and peers' are given.

Related goals: 2, 3, 5, 6, 9

All about me: Special days (pages 58-59)

An ongoing project suggestion that encourages children to celebrate the good in each other. Self-confidence and self-esteem are discussed. Several steps are taken towards the Early Learning Goals during the course of this activity.

Related goals: 2, 3, 8, 12, 14

People who help us: Families (pages 60-61)

Exploring the make-up of families, extended, blended and original! Stepping stones for the goal 'understand that they can expect others to treat their own needs, views, cultures and beliefs with respect' are included.

Related goals: 2, 3, 9, 14

Planning chart

Personal, Social and Emotional Development	ELG 1	ELG 2	ELG 3	ELG 4	ELG 5	ELG 6	ELG 7	ELG 8	ELG 9	ELG 10	ELG 11	ELG 12	ELG 13	ELG14
Circle time	✓	✓	✓	✓	✓			✓			✓	✓		✓
Choosing time	✓	✓	✓	✓		✓								
The home corner	✓	✓	✓	✓		✓	✓	✓	✓			✓		
Learning to share		✓	✓	✓					✓	✓	✓	✓		✓
Wait for it!	✓	✓		✓				✓	✓			✓		✓
Facing up to fears					✓	✓							✓	
Mirror faces												✓	✓	✓
Travelling Tara	✓		✓	✓	✓				✓	✓				✓
Dressing games			✓				✓							
Celebrating cultures and beliefs	✓	✓		✓		✓	✓	✓	✓	✓			✓	
Seasons: Seasonal celebrations & traditions		✓	✓	✓	✓	✓		✓	✓				✓	✓
Water: Working together with water						✓					✓			
Colour: Colours of the world		✓	✓		✓				✓					
All about me: Special days		✓	✓					✓				✓		✓
People who help us: Families		✓	✓						✓					✓